THE PHYSICALLY HANDICAPPED
An Annotated Bibliography of Empirical Research Studies, 1970–1979

William A. Pearman
Philip Starr

GARLAND PUBLISHING, INC. • NEW YORK & LONDON
1981

© 1981 William A. Pearman and Philip Starr
All rights reserved

Library of Congress Cataloging in Publication Data
Pearman, William A., 1940–
  The physically handicapped.

  (Garland reference library of social science ; v. 76)
  Includes indexes.
  1. Physically handicapped—Bibliography. 2. Physically handicapped—Psychology—Bibliography. 3. Physically handicapped—Public opinion—Bibliography.
  I. Starr, Philip, 1935–   . II. Title. III. Series.
  Z6675.R4P4 [RD797]   016.3624   80-8503
  ISBN 0-8240-9484-0   AACR2

Printed on acid-free, 250-year-life paper
Manufactured in the United States of America

CONTENTS

Preface	vii
Measurement and Methodological Problems in Physical Disability Research	ix
The Studies	1
Journals Searched	119
Indexes	
Subject Index	123
Index of Second Authors	129

PREFACE

This volume represents a significant step toward reducing the gap between social research and the delivery of services to the physically disabled. The book both summarizes research findings and provides annotated references to important studies in the physical disability field.

Intended as a tool for clinicians in the day-to-day performance of their professional responsibilities, the book, in the review section, summarizes trends in the research materials to assist clinicians in finding help in solving pressing problems.

Researchers will also find useful the summary of the state of sociological and behavioral science knowledge about physical disability and the indication of areas in which further research is needed. This book can be used by researchers to continue to develop and expand the knowledge base upon which practice rests, and to spare them the necessity of "reinventing the wheel" for each case, problem, or challenge they face.

Many decisions had to be made by the authors at the start of this project. The field disability is enormous; it can be defined in many ways, depending on one's disciplinary perspective and experiences. We chose to treat only physical disability, excluding the related areas of psychological and learning disabilities, and to limit ourselves to the findings of empirical research studies published in a broad grouping of medical, education, and social and behavioral science journals. Thus, we excluded materials based upon impression or unplanned observation as well as library or armchair research studies and literature reviews. The list of journals searched follows the bibliography section. Because of the number of journals on our list and our desire to present the most current findings possible, we limited the studies to be reviewed to those published from 1970 to 1979. Those studies that best met the authors' criteria are listed and annotated. Obviously, many materials were excluded. However, in the face of the demand for summary and synthesis that exists in the clinical, research, and administrative worlds that deal with the physically disabled, the authors feel that certain exclusions are necessary and legitimate.

This book would not have been possible without the understanding and support of our home institutions, the H.K. Cooper Clinic of Lancaster, Pennsylvania, and Millersville State College, Millersville, Pennsylvania. For the junior author, it is also based on experiences supported in part by the National Institute of Dental Research, National Institute of Health. Many excellent and dedicated librarians aided us in our search for resource materials. Libraries used in our work include: the Helen Ganser Library of Millersville State College, the Milton S. Hershey Medical Library of the Pennsylvania State University, the Welch Medical Library of Johns Hopkins University, the State Library of Pennsylvania, the Library of the Medical School of the University of Maryland, the Hillman Library and the Library of the Graduate School of Public Health at the University of Pittsburgh, the Point Park College Library, the Pennsylvania State University Library, the Temple University Library, the Library of the Medical School of New York University, and the New York Academy of Medicine Library.

MEASUREMENT AND METHODOLOGICAL PROBLEMS IN PHYSICAL DISABILITY RESEARCH

In the broad field of physical disability there is little research dealing with measurement of the central concept. This contributes significantly to the lack of organization and direction in the field. Not only is there a neglect of questions dealing with validity and reliability of important concepts in the field; there is also evidence that definitions and interpretations differ according to the individual researcher's discipline, perspective, training, and work experience. There is a lack of theoretical models that draw together previous research findings as well as a lack of causal modeling.

There is little agreement between conceptual and operational measures about the term "disability." Definitions of disability vary according to sex and race (item 40) as well as age of the respondent (item 41). This must change if there is to be substantial progress in research or an effective public policy relative to disability (item 100). Reports citing statistical information relative to incidence and severity of disability will be viewed with suspicion, and comparisons between states or countries will be rendered less meaningful, unless agreement can be reached on definitions.

As we reviewed the literature, we became aware of the interchangeability of terms in the field. Such terms as disability, disfigurement, impairment, and handicap may be used to describe separate and distinct concepts. One study we reviewed did demonstrate the independence in variance for the indices of disability (item 201). Nevertheless, we decided to treat all these as the same concept. Otherwise, we would have had to produce several books, rather than one, in order to cover the field. Furthermore, we feel that there are more similarities between the concepts than differences.

In addition to the definitional problems in the field, there is confusion arising from misdiagnosis and the variability in diagnostic measures and rehabilitation success criteria employed by clinicians and practitioners. The frequency of misdiagnosis of clients is one problem; in one study, counselors who reevaluated their original intake diagnosis showed a mean agreement with themselves of only 65.7% (item 10). The extent, severity, and implications of this problem need to be documented.

Variability due to the employment of different measures of rehabilitation success also merits investigation. Some research has been conducted to determine the degree to which functioning of these various criteria is interrelated (item 3). This research examined indicators of both physical and social functioning. There was a high degree of correlation between the indicators of physical functioning; they were moderately related to assessments of social functioning, and less related to self-administered indicators of social functioning. This research highlights not only the need for better measures of social functioning but also the need for researchers to focus on similar dimensions of social functioning.

Many studies to be discussed in other sections of this essay deal with the ability of given scales to predict rehabilitation success or to measure disability. However, there has been little use of such statistical techniques as factor analysis to probe more deeply into the nature of these scales. One exception concerns factor analysis of the Disability Factor Scales (item 138).

One of the most impressive causal models of disability deals with three types of factors: agent, host, and environmental (item 308). Each factor in this model contains a number of subfactors. Although directed specifically to the industrial and occupational medicine world and its special problems, this model illustrates the broadly applicable utility of combining several variables to examine such problems as risk of severe disability. It is also a relatively comprehensive attempt to construct a paradigm of the field of disability research.

To date, we have a collection of empirical facts and Wan's preliminary efforts at establishing a comprehensive paradigm. Additional research, starting from clearer definitions of handicap, and studies involving a host of factors are needed before the field can move beyond its present stage of development.

One final note: several researchers have focused their attention in a specific area, for example, Richardson (items 231-236), who concentrated on children and their perceptions and acceptance of handicapped children, and Starr (items 274-277), who concentrated on social functioning of children with cleft lip and/or palate. Based on our review of the literature, this appears to be the most effective way for knowledge-building to occur. Otherwise, we are left with numerous, but isolated, research findings from which to make sense.

FACTORS RELATED TO REHABILITATION SUCCESS

Rehabilitation is the process by which an individual is restored to health or returned to former levels of capacity. Central concerns of the field of physical rehabilitation must be: How is rehabilitation facilitated and what factors are related to success.

Because of its broadness and the possibility of many interpretations, the term "rehabilitation" is elusive. Its meaning varies with the patient's or client's perception, the discipline and training of the practitioner, the handicap or disease in question, and various other factors. As indicated below, there are many indicators of rehabilitation success. However, there appears to be some agreement among these measures (item 3). This is particularly true for indicators of physical functioning.

It is not possible to predict exactly what will occur in any given case of disability. However, researchers have developed generalized models that describe stages of recovery. One model is based on information on adult males following primary myocardial infarction (item 117). That model not only describes changes in concept of self at each stage of rehabilitation, but also stresses sequential tasks that need to be accomplished at each stage. Overall, the stages are viewed as a socialization process. They focus on facing reality, experimenting, and reorganizing the psychic image. An important part of the rehabilitation process involves the patient's or client's ability to assume the sick role at the proper time, but then to relinquish that role when necessary. Denial of disability may facilitate rehabilitation in the beginning stages of an individual's illness, but a realistic acceptance of one's disability must eventually be attained if long-term success is to be achieved (item 128).

A number of studies have focused on identifying factors favorable to rehabilitation. Generally, these studies have concentrated on specific types of handicap or disability, for example, arthritis (item 301), blindness (item 152), hearing impairment (item 141), myocardial infarction (item 202), and spinal injury (item 133). As will become apparent in our discussion of factors related to successful rehabilitation, a facilitating factor in one type of disability can be a negative factor in another type. Although we emphasize the need for a multiple-factor model applicable across disability states, the attainment of such may be an impossibility. We must also bear in mind that factors that foster one aspect of rehabilitation, for example, return to work, do not simultaneously foster all other aspects of rehabilitation. They may even pull in opposite directions. A spirit of personal independence may foster individual achievement, but may work against reintegration into social groups.

One variable identified in numerous studies is the attitude of the patient toward rehabilitation, for example, the desire to be well, to relinquish the sick role. In a study of productivity of spinal-cord-injured patients it was found that the most productive patients were those who developed goals for themselves, were forward-looking, and paid minimal attention to their physical loss (item 133). In a study of persons with cancer of the larynx, a realistic attitude and an optimistic rehabilitation outlook were identified as important success factors (item 91). Further support for this position is provided in a study of post-myocardial infarction patients in which all patients with a negative attitude toward their illness and prognosis did poorly, while those with positive attitudes did well (item 202).

An important aspect of attitudinal state is the psychosocial functioning of the patient prior to the onset of disability; for example, persons who successfully survived open-heart surgery regarded sick persons in a negative way, regarded themselves as independent and active, and exhibited pre-operative tendencies to reject the sick role (item 29). Objective factors such as amount of work involvement prior to sickness (item 84) or, as in the case of laryngectomized patients, level of prior speech proficiency (item 132) are also important indicators of a patient's chances for successful rehabilitation.

One psycho-social factor that receives much attention in the literature is IQ. It was found to be a factor in the rehabilitation of patients with chronic rheumatoid arthritis. Among this group, individuals with higher IQ's were more likely to maintain functional performance and exhibit improved social adjustment (item 301). In a study on mobility-skill acquisition among the blind, intelligence was concluded to be a factor in terms of rate of skill acquisition, but level of acquisition was not a function of IQ (item 152).

Intelligence may be a factor that discriminates between persisters and dropouts in rehabilitative processes; this was documented for vocational rehabilitation programs (item 292). Researchers and clinicians need to remember that intelligence is a broad concept of many subcomponents or dimensions. Some of these may be important for some disabilities but not for others. For example, the ability to think creatively has been demonstrated as important for the return to productivity of spinal-cord-injured patients (item 133), but is probably not a factor in some other disabilities. This brings up again the question of what rehabilitation means--does it mean a return to productivity, or does it mean, for example, learning to cope with a facial scar?

A number of studies have examined the impact of age on rehabilitation. Generally, the younger the patient, the better the chances for success (items 87, 112, 133, 141). However, in a study of speech proficiency among laryngectomized patients, we are cautioned that although age may be an important factor in individual cases, it is not as important to success in learning esophageal speech as earlier work suggested (item 132).

Studies in which subjects are classified simply as old or young may provide conclusions different from those studies in which more refined age breakdowns are provided. For example, examination of children recovering from head injuries revealed that intellectual recovery was best predicted by age, with older children--those over ten--scoring higher than younger children (item 323).

Special attention should also be given to the impact of adolescence on the rehabilitative process. Among patients on hemodialysis, adolescents followed medical regimens less well than adults, had a significantly lower vocational rehabilitation, and had more restricted social activities (item 58). It must be remembered that each age group has its own particular concerns, for example, independent functioning for the elderly, social integration for teenagers, and sexual functioning for young adults, and chronic disease or permanent injury can aggravate these "normal" stresses.

Socioeconomic characteristics are important in the rehabilitation process to the extent that they foster patient comfort, contribute to the ability to obtain therapy or treatment, or otherwise aid in coping with disability-associated problems (item 206). In vocational rehabilitation, patients of higher socioeconomic background return to work earlier (item 84). Caution must be exercised in drawing conclusions about the relationship of social class and rehabilitation, however, because workers from the higher social classes or those with a large number of dependents may be targeted to receive special services or training to help them return to work (item 295).

The findings on the importance of education, a factor often associated with attainment of higher socioeconomic status, indicate that individuals with high educational attainment are good candidates for various types of rehabilitation (items 1, 9, 132).

Involvement of a supportive family in a patient's rehabilitation is significant. Families can help reinforce cooperation with medical regimens and can provide emotional support. It is important that in encouraging the patient, the parent or family act, not out of role expectations that invoke authority relations, but out of respect for the patient as a person. Support for this argument can be derived from a study of epileptic children and their families (item 105). Positive pressures from significant others have been documented as a factor in the patient's return to work (item 84), and one that can be changed by therapeutic intervention.

Successful rehabilitation efforts have been linked to the timeliness of treatment. The earlier the treatment, the greater likelihood of success. This has been documented by several studies (item 57, 87, 90).

The relation of race to rehabilitation needs more attention. We know that blacks have a higher mortality rate following myocardial infarction than do whites (item 263), but we do not have a clear understanding of why this is so. Race has been identified as significant in other types of disabilities as well. For example, it is related to rehabilitation outcomes among young adults with hearing impairment: that is, white hearing-impaired clients had higher potential for rehabilitation than hearing-impaired clients of other racial groups. Many studies did not utilize racially representative samples, so their ability to assess the effects of race on rehabilitation is limited. Caution must be exercised in generalizing on race, since professional perceptions of patients may be influenced by race.

Various studies have assembled information intended to increase accuracy in predicting rehabilitation success. Through the use of psychometric predictors, it was demonstrated that prediction of success by hemiplegics is possible at program outset (item 14). Predictability improves as more information is included in the regression equation (item 23). Even if success cannot be predicted completely, research of this type could suggest which behaviors need to be modified for rehabilitation to take place (item 315).

The Minnesota Multiphasic Personality Inventory (MMPI) has been employed as a predictive device. Use of this test on a regular basis is not recommended (item 75), but benefits of restricted usage, such as predicting psychosocial adaptation to cancer, have been documented (item 273). Other tests have also been employed with some success (item 120).

While identifying factors that contribute to successful rehabilitation, research has also pinpointed factors that are obstacles to rehabilitation. Generally, the obstacles vary with the disability being studied. However, there are some general findings. For example, denial is an ineffective coping strategy for handicapped groups (items 34, 276), long inactivity prior to the start of rehabilitation is a disadvantage (items 87, 90), length of hospitalization has no effect on improved coping (item 76), failure may be due to lack of medical knowledge (item 187). Severe organic and psychological problems were cited by many studies as a cause of failure.

Finally, we wish to stress that not all of the disabled will welcome or cooperate with attempts at rehabilitation. Some will view rehabilitation as impractical for them. Among black-lung miners this attitude was associated with severe organic pathology (respiratory), advanced middle age, limited education and work background, more rural residence, and unwillingness to geographically relocate (item 11). Intervention in such cases is most difficult, and calls for a multifaceted approach.

In this section we have identified various factors related to rehabilitation outcomes. Given this knowledge, we should be able to screen clients on their chances for rehabilitation success. We need to use our knowledge to construct better, more sophisticated predictive models. Much of our current knowledge is based on such simplistic techniques as correlational models.

SELF-ACCEPTANCE OF DISABILITY

The sociological concept of "sick role" requires that the ill individual admit to having a problem that requires intervention or help from an appropriate medical or healthcare professional. The concept also assumes that a person's illness is temporary and that the individual desires to recover from it.

Two criticisms can be leveled at this concept. First, a person's ill health may not be temporary, as in the case of amputees or patients with cleft lip and/or palate. Therefore, the important question is what factors facilitate or inhibit acceptance by the individual of his or her ill health.

Second, individuals are not always aware that they are ill; symptoms are not always apparent. Some individuals seek diagnosis or advice only to discredit the diagnosis or deny the abnormality or diagnosed pathology. Others do not even seek help, but simply deny their disabilities. At whatever stage it occurs, denial is not a successful mechanism for adjustment to disability.

Denial of disability may have an initial psychological benefit for the handicapped individual, but it must be integrated gradually with a concept of disability. This will allow the rehabilitation process to occur (item 128). It would be helpful for clinicians to be able to identify patterns of reaction to disability. Such identification is sometimes possible on an individual basis (item 178). The study discussed in item 178, which dealt with myocardial infarction cases, also demonstrated that there is a degree of continuity in reaction patterns throughout the convalescent period.

More research is needed on the process by which individuals move from denial to acceptance of disability. A beginning can be found in a longitudinal study of crippled children aged five to nine (item 191). These children progressed from a realization that the handicap would not disappear, to severe depression, to hesitant but gradual incorporation of the disability into their self-concept.

The process of denial among the handicapped can be viewed as a form of stigma management. This concept was described in a study of amputees, but regarded as ineffective (item 34). Denial was also described as an unsatisfactory coping technique for teenagers with cleft conditions (item 276). Where prosthetic devices are needed, denial serves as a negative factor in adjusting to the device (item 200).

Characteristics of deniers and nondeniers were identified in a study of post-myocardial infarction patients (item 50). Deniers were more likely to be from non-Anglo ethnic groups (Jewish and Italian) rather than of Anglo origins (British and Irish). Not only did the deniers differ from nondeniers in disavowing physical problems, they also denied possessing unfavorable personality traits. This study also noted the persistence of the denial response phenomenon. Another study reported on the role of denial in protecting the patient from frustration and despair (item 153). This study examined denial and self-image in patients with various handicaps. The order in which patients relied on denial, from highest to lowest, was stroke, lung cancer, and heart patients.

One of the most comprehensive studies on the acceptance of disability focused on the sociopsychological characteristics of the physically disabled (item 286). In this study, which dealt with amputees, twenty-seven client characteristics were treated as independent variables. Only three of the twenty-seven were statistically significant factors to higher acceptance scores. They were: years of education (higher educated), religious preference (Catholic), and occupational category (sales and clerical).

In a study of males with sudden traumatic injury, personality patterns were viewed as important determinants of reaction to disability (item 128). Subjects who possessed a cognitive style marked by tolerance of the uncertain or unstable were better able to integrate notions of disability into their self-concept than were intolerant subjects. The importance of personality in acceptance of handicap was reinforced in a study of stutterers (item 269). High self-esteem and positive self-concept are among personality variables most often identified (items 158, 276). Not only are personality disturbances related to denial or nonacceptance of handicap, they also have implications for compliance with therapy and medical regimens (item 139).

Adequate explanation by medical or therapeutic staff reinforced by a supportive family atmosphere can contribute to an intellectual understanding of sickness or disability. This latter factor was shown to be related to acceptance and compliance (item 200).

Acceptance may be related to the interaction of factors that deal with the specific nature of the problems posed by the disability and personal attributes of the disabled. For example, a study on adolescents and chronic hemodialysis noted difficulties posed for adolescents because of the creation of stress in areas problematic for that age group (item 58).

Acceptance is further related to societal reaction to the specific handicap and how that handicap is perceived. Self-acceptance as handicapped may be more difficult for those individuals who suffer from a nonvisible disability or from a condition not clearly defined as a handicap by society. Those with characteristics of impairment that clearly indicate sickness or impairment tended to have better interpersonal relationships. A clear label leads to greater self-acceptance and subsequent social acceptance (item 330). However, in some cases where individuals were clearly labeled as disabled, for example, lepers, the stigma was so great that even after successful treatment, they avoided social or interpersonal contact (item 19). That acceptance of one's disability is related to the social context has been demonstrated for hard of hearing children (item 163). In this case, interaction with the nonhearing-impaired influenced the social behavior of the hard of hearing child in ways thought to enhance self-acceptance.

The disabled might be more accepting of their state than we realize. This was documented in a survey of participants in the Illinois White House Conference on the Handicapped (item 313). A majority of the respondents considered their disability a fact of life and did not wish that they were no longer disabled. Acceptance of disability is desirable because it has consequences for behavioral functioning and the individual's psychological and social adjustment (items 268, 275). In order for individuals to accept their disability, they must be aware of it. Attempts are often made to hide chronic diseases from patients. The effect of awareness is an unresolved question; it may benefit some patients but not others (item 96). Lack of action due to nonawareness is not the same as denial.

In this section we have shown that acceptance of disability is a complicated mechanism involving various psychological and social variables. The impact of a given variable differs with the individual, his condition, and the environment in which he operates.

REACTIONS OF SIGNIFICANT OTHERS

Handicapped individuals do not live in a vacuum, but are part of a larger environment. The reactions of others can be important in forming the self-concept of the handicapped as well as contributing to or inhibiting return to optimal functioning.

Reaction to the handicapped depends on contextual variables, personality variables, demographic factors, and so on. Of course there are exceptions to most generalizations in social science research, but certain patterns have been discovered that characterize social reaction to the handicapped; these patterns were summarized in a study of the social attitudes of university students toward the disabled (item 254). The findings were that previous and frequent contact with the handicapped leads to more favorable attitudes toward them; females have more positive attitudes toward the handicapped than males do; individuals in the helping professions have a higher rate of tolerance toward the handicapped than others; persons with mild disabilities and less visible handicaps are more likely to receive acceptance than persons with other types of handicaps; relationships of the nonhandicapped with the handicapped are likely to be characterized by low intensity and be fleeting or temporary as opposed to permanent.

Numerous studies have demonstrated that there is a hierarchy of societal responses toward the handicapped. In general, the hierarchy of attitude preference is: physically disabled, sensorily disabled, mentally disabled (items 104, 289). Some studies offered the response "socially disabled," for example, alcoholics; when this option was provided, this group ranked lowest (item 99, 289). As will be noted below, numerous studies have demonstrated subhierarchies within these broad classes. A longitudinal study has demonstrated stability of preference in attitudes regardless of the demographic characteristics of the sample and the type of measuring instrument used (item 104).

In reviewing the literature, we find various studies in which professionals have been asked to rank disabilities on such criteria as the degree of disturbance the disability presents them with, how they feel society reacts to the disability, or their own personal fears about the disability. Health professionals felt that disabilities dealing with motor ability were more disturbing than disabilities dealing with cranial or systemic disorders (item 118). In this study, an array of physical conditions were presented as stimuli. Blindness was most disturbing, stomach ulcers were considered least disturbing. Nursing students ranked disabilities according to how disturbing they would be to them if they personally were to incur the disability (item 199). Their ranking of eight conditions listed complete blindness as most disturbing and amputation of the arm above the elbow as least disturbing. Their reasons for ranking provide general insight into the structure of the hierarchies of disability: conditions with which one can learn to cope were favored over conditions to which one has only the alternative of succumbing; nonfatal conditions were viewed as less disturbing than fatal conditions; isolating diseases were perceived as more disturbing than nonisolating diseases.

The presence of negative attitudes can hurt people. For example, males who lisp were rated as lower than nonlispers in speaking ability, intelligence, education, masculinity, and friendship (item 198). Professionals must become aware of and deal with negative attitudes toward disability groups. There can be little question that these attitudes influence the client regardless of how well the client is functioning.

A number of experiments have been conducted in situations in which normals are likely to render help to the handicapped. One study found that certain kinds of handicaps are more likely to evoke sympathetic responses, for example, bandages around the forearm bring more positive responses to the wearer than eye patches or scars (item 247). This experiment also demonstrated that when subjects are made to feel responsible for the role player's accident, more help is offered. Handicapped people are avoided in interpersonal situations if the other actor perceives the situation as having a cost for him (item 298). The nature of the situation, that is, whether or not the handicap creates a high dependence for the individual, has also been shown to be important in the other's offer of help (item 9).

The personality of the nonhandicapped person influences his or her perception of the handicapped. Subjects high in intolerance of ambiguity scored high in negative attitude toward the disabled regardless of the disability type being rated, while tolerant subjects' responses were more affected by disability type (item 81). Aggression as a personality variable has also been shown to be negatively related to positive attitudes toward the disabled (item 71), and high anxiety levels are associated with negative attitudes (item 293). The research dealing with personality factors influencing perception of the handicapped suggests that a segment of the population finds it easier to avoid the handicapped person.

From the perspective of labeling theory, if a person is clearly defined as deviant or handicapped, others will tend to avoid him or her or to see only the negative features of the person. One intensive study noted exception to this. That study found that characteristics that clearly indicate impairment tend to be associated with better interpersonal relationships and that the more severely impaired are likely to have better interpersonal relations than the less severely impaired (item 330). This questions the labeling perspective by suggesting that when the deviant aspect is known, is defined as deviant or different by all parties, then social interaction proceeds more smoothly.

Social reactions to the handicapped are also influenced by the handicapped person's life history. For example, in a simulation study, Israeli disabled veterans were rated higher than other handicapped persons in terms of social functioning (item 130). This is understandable when one recognizes the high status accorded the military in the social scheme of Israel.

Sometimes other attributes of the handicapped person become more dominant in interpersonal relationships. Race is an example of one such variable (item 129). The white person, in both the handicapped and nonhandicapped situation, was favored over the black person.

One study posed questions concerning the effect that minority status has on one's perception of the handicapped. This study asked whether a cultural minority (Asian students in the United States) would exhibit more positive attitudes toward the disabled than a majority group exhibited (item

293). The results indicated more sympathy from the majority (American) respondents.

There is mixed evidence as to how the handicapped themselves view other handicapped individuals. In a study of university students, handicapped and nonhandicapped students did not differ in their attitudes toward the handicapped (item 151). Another study suggested that distinctions are made between relatively visible handicaps and relatively invisible handicaps. Those handicapped people with more visible handicaps had more positive attitudes toward other handicapped people (item 63). The study suggested that promoting opportunities for association with persons with like handicaps might be beneficial for those with visible handicaps, but less beneficial for those with less visible handicaps.

Just as in other social situations, such as ethnic and racial integration, perception of attitudinal similarity results in increased attractiveness of the disabled to the nondisabled (item 6). Numerous studies have demonstrated that reactions and attitudes toward the handicapped can be influenced in a positive direction. Special instruction or lectures have been successful with children, college students, and adults (items 88, 127, 148, 149). Videotape presentations (item 245) and videotape along with live presentations have been shown to have positive impact (item 64). One study reported on successful use of hypnosis in changing attitudes toward the handicapped (item 54).

Generally, information helps to improve attitudes. However, in one study which dealt with business and professional men's receptivity to laryngectomized workers, information also contributed to the development of an unwillingness to place the subject in certain public contact positions (item 88).

If stereotyping is reduced by the presentation of favorable information about disabled people, does presentation of negative information serve to reinforce stereotyping and elicit unfavorable attitudes? No support was found for this suggestion (item 95).

In underdeveloped areas of the world, which often exhibit high rates of disabilities because of lack of medical personnel and professional services, the problem of changing attitudes is a special one. It has been shown that even in areas of low literacy attitude change can be effected. Special processes that rely on literate change agents have been identified (item 174).

Another question is whether nonhandicapped individuals distinguish levels of severity or subconditions within a given disability. A clue comes from a study which asked if sighted people respond to different levels of visual loss (item 72). Respondents did not differentiate the partially sighted from the totally sightless.

At several points we have referred to the importance of attitudes of significant others. Let us examine these attitudes from a developmental perspective. The first significant others for any human being are family members. A disabled child affects the family and its life style (item 27). Some parents, especially the mothers, become overprotective of the child. For example, a study of children who were burn victims noted that their mothers had a high need to "mother" them (item 170). A "vulnerable child syndrome" has been identified (item 260). This is marked largely by high concern and is viewed as a result of disturbances in the parent-child relationship following early childhood illness. Some parents have a slightly different reaction and begin to withdraw from the handicapped child when the child is not making normal progress (item 137).

Often the professionals attending the handicapped child give negative cues to the parent by withdrawing or seeming to lose interest. This raises interesting questions about the influence of staff reactions on parents and their subsequent interactions with their handicapped child. Specifically it raises the question of how a professional reacts to client problems in order to help the parents maintain hope, but also develop realistic expectations.

Normally, the position of parents as "significant others" is gradually replaced somewhat by the child's peers. Research indicates that children's understanding of disability does not occur until approximately four years of age (items 124, 311). Thus it would appear that this age is a good time to educate children in proper attitudes. Generally, children prefer to play and interact with able-bodied friends. This is true of both handicapped and nonhandicapped children (items 218, 252). There may be some handicaps that are exceptions to this, for example, stuttering (item 320).

Children's attitudes toward their handicapped peers seem to change over time. One study suggests that values change until they resemble those of the parent of the same sex. This occurs by grade twelve (item 231). The study suggests that values at earlier age levels are not acquired from parents. For boys, peer-group values are important determinants of their behavior and attitudes toward the handicapped, and this peer influence increases with age (item 235). The same study did not view peers as exerting similar influence on girls and their value acquisition.

In their evaluation of handicapped children girls place a high emphasis on cosmetic effects and show a greater dislike for children with facial disfigurement and the obese, while boys demonstrate a lower preference for children with functional handicaps (item 231). One study suggested that it is boys who change the most attitudinally as a result of integrated school exposure to handicapped children (item 225). Children do not seem to differ from adults in their hierarchical ratings of types of disabilities.

As with the general population, attitude change may be possible among children, but only in situations in which very extensive and intimate contact occurs are the disabled seen as fairly similar to able-bodied children (item 312). Length of exposure may be a factor (item 67).

Attitudes of professionals toward the disabled are important service-delivery factors and must be dealt with both during training and on the job. Deficiencies in knowledge have been noted among professionals who are beginning work with various groups of handicapped people (item 146). Generally, it is felt that knowledge in such situations is associated with previous contact or exposure to the disabling condition (item 146). Anxiety and other feelings such as frustrations and guilt seem to be associated with lack of previous contact (item 309). Previous contact, however, does not appear to be the answer to all professional-client problems in this area. The attribution of negative personality traits by speech clinicians to stutterers was not related to previous clinical contact, that is, previous contact did not result in the attribution of more positive traits (item 296). Sometimes exposure has a negative effect on the service provider (item 60).

New professionals find their first encounters with the disabled especially difficult. However, as one study notes, they adjust expectations of perfection to realistic ones (item 223). As in the general population, attitudes and behaviors of professionals are influenced by a number of factors including personality (item 167) and degree of effectiveness in work (item 46).

As a final group of significant others, let us look at teachers and their reactions to the handicapped. Evidence indicates that educators have negative feelings toward handicapped children, regardless of the type of institutional setting or the professional status of the educator (item 98).

There is evidence that teachers operate on cultural stereotypes relating physical unattractiveness to decreased intellectual abilities and vice-versa (items 39, 238). As compared to students, teachers have a broader definition of the term "disability" (item 272). In one study, college faculty seemed quite willing to admit handicapped students to their classes, but did express some reservations concerning blind and deaf students (item 205).

Findings on the influence of integrated classroom exposure to the disabled, at least to the blind, are ambiguous. Both positive reports and reports of no difference exist (items 131, 140).

The social context of the labeling process is so delicate that professionals must be on guard against fostering deviant negative identities among their clients or patients. How this operates has been described for physical therapist-patient information (item 154).

Parents, peers, and professional service providers are all significant others. Their reactions both attitudinally and behaviorally are important factors in the rehabilitation of the handicapped. In providing therapy and counseling we must remember that simply treating the individual without reference to the broader social context will not ensure long-term rehabilitation success. Clinicians must learn how to use the positive factors identified above and how to help their clients overcome or deal with the negative factors.

EMPLOYABILITY OF THE HANDICAPPED

Questions concerning the employability of the handicapped can be approached on at least three levels: the societal, representing the view of the larger society toward the potential productive contributions of the handicapped; the organizational or institutional level, which deals with the experiences of the handicapped in specific occupations or with specific organizations or employers; and the individual level, which deals with the attitudes, motivations, and experiences of the handicapped individual. There is much information available concerning vocational rehabilitation and the attitudes of both employers and the handicapped, but such data deal with individual or idiosyncratic experiences from which it is difficult to generalize.

From a societal perspective, industrial societies such as the United States value individuals for the contribution they can make to the increased productivity of the system. Those unable to make productive contributions are perceived as of lower status and of less value than the more productive. The handicapped who do successfully enter the job market often find that expectations of lessened or non-productivity precede them.

Can employers' expectations of the handicapped be influenced? One study demonstrated that introductory material on the particular handicap might help to increase employers' expectations. However, increased information can also lead the employer to narrowly define the types of jobs for which the potential employee is eligible (item 88). A pre- and post-attitudinal test to determine the impact of an intensive educational campaign on employers' attitudes toward employment of epileptics indicated no differences. Employer resistance was identified as the major factor contributing to underemployment of epileptics (item 248).

Research has demonstrated that certain groups of employers are more willing to hire the handicapped: the young (item 7), larger firms, manufacturing firms, and those with previous experience with the disabled (item 97).

A number of factors associated with success by the handicapped in the job market have been identified. These factors include: less serious or less visible handicap (item 242), at least a high school education (items 8, 162, 207, 208, 302), a realistic self-concept and/or motivation to work (item 195), being married (items 162, 302), completion of specialized vocational training programs or workshops (items 22, 52, 208, 242). These factors allow identification of clients or patients who can be targeted for specialized vocational rehabilitation.

Once disabled employees are hired, employers seem to be quite satisfied with their performance (item 294). The same research indicates that the disabled employees themselves express moderate job satisfaction and have good attitudes toward both work and self. However, they seem to overestimate their personal qualities in comparison to their employers' judgments. Just as it is significant in obtaining employment, a realistic self-concept is significant in terms of attitude toward work. Employers and nonhandicapped co-workers are often surprised by the solid work performances of handicapped employees (item 12).

The disabled who do find employment seem to perform well and to be stable employees (items 216, 226). However, they do not generally achieve advancement as rapidly as the nonhandicapped and often receive lower salaries for comparable work (item 226). The occupational history of the handicapped seems to be comparable to that of their nonhandicapped siblings (items 185, 226). This suggests that family background may be an important variable in the occupational achievement of the handicapped.

One researcher identified job classifications in which the disabled might find employment (item 220). The danger in this approach is that the handicapped might confine themselves to these job possibilities, or that employers might rely on such lists for placement purposes and not open up more avenues for advancement.

The handicapped generally exhibit a high level of dependency in applying for and obtaining jobs (item 226). They and significant others associated with them are somewhat unaware of available employment (item 279). A study of job-seeking patterns among the deaf noted that they often sell themselves short; few utilize employment agencies in their search, and when they do, they are more likely to utilize agencies specializing in blue-collar placements (item 33).

A related question concerns return to work by individuals who suffered disabilities after they had established themselves in the labor market. Again, positive self-concept is an important factor. In a study of spinal-cord-injured patients five years after the onset of injury, the most productive were forward-looking individuals with a high number of goals who paid minimal attention to their physical loss (item 133).

Similar findings are reported for a group of post-myocardial infarction patients. Their post-myocardial involvement was related to their involvement pre-myocardial infarction (item 84). This study also identified as important variables in return to work the patient's perception of health status, social class, feeling of control over fate, and feeling of pressure from significant others. Family pressure seems to be important in both initial employment and return to it, a fact to be kept in mind by clinicians. A realistic, sympathetic, but not patronizing picture of physical limitation is needed by the disabled individual who contemplates return to work. Perception of physical limits is likely to influence the desire to return to work (item 143).

A study on women in long-term hemodialysis concluded that in the work ethic, men are encouraged to maintain careers more than women are, and women seem to substitute home for career. This is especially true if women have competing responsibilities. Single employed women continued their work schedules with minimal disruption, whereas working wives felt time constraints and returned to the home (item 94). These findings demonstrate the extra pressures brought by disability. Indeed, strong feelings of self-worth are needed to meet and conquer these pressures.

Do handicapped individuals differ from normals in vocational aspirations? Data on blind children indicate that they have high but not unrealistic aspirations. However, they doubt that they will achieve what they would like (item 115). In a comparison of adolescents with cystic fibrosis and a control group of adolescents, the patient group scored lower than the controls in both vocational and educational aspirations (item 93). In the same study the patient group scored significantly higher in relation to commitment to work, work values, and awareness of occupational information. More research is needed to determine the reasons for these findings. Since they might anticipate discrimination in employment, do the handicapped heighten their values in this area, or do they stress work as a replacement for other social outlets?

In this section we have noted the importance of personality variables such as a strong self-concept and a realistic assessment of one's ability as aids to employment by the handicapped. At the same time, we noted that there may be environmental factors such as prejudice or ignorance that work against the handicapped in their pursuit of work. Again, we conclude by stressing the need to develop a comprehensive view of all factors involved.

THE IMPORTANCE OF PHYSICAL ATTRACTIVENESS

Although sociologists have not been in agreement as to the core of the American value system, they have generally agreed that Americans tend to emphasize values associated with youth, physical attractiveness, and the pursuit of beauty. This combination of values has special meaning for a group of individuals who fail by reason of disability or disfigurement to meet the exacting criteria of the majority group of society.

Much research has been conducted on the importance of physical attractiveness and its impact on various areas of social life. Societal reaction to physical attractiveness impacts first on the participants or actors themselves. In our society this reaction deeply affects the physically disabled, especially those with visible signs of disfigurement.

Physical appearance is particularly important during adolescence, a time when dating and overt sexual behavior normally begin and when self-concepts and identity undergo heightened introspection. Evidence indicates that handicapped adolescents report a greater dissatisfaction with physical appearance than nonhandicapped adolescents. Females, in particular, report unhappiness and dissatisfaction (item 126). Unhappiness and dissatisfaction interact with other factors such as school success and anxiety (item 126). The exact nature of this interaction is not yet known.

As adults, these individuals may continue to have a negative self-concept. In our sex-oriented society the disabled and disfigured again form an at-risk group. Research has shown that this group feel themselves to be less positive as males or females, with the more severely disabled or disfigured having the least positive self sex-role assessment (item 268).

Some observers have identified the phenomenon of reverse isolation, that is, failure to participate in or return to society even when factors indicate a readiness to do so (item 19). The stigma of physical disfigurement remains an indelible aspect of self-concept; it reaches into many aspects of life. It not only affects interpersonal relationships but other areas as well, for example, career planning and vocational choice (item 91).

We stated above that females are particularly vulnerable to the emphasis on physical attractiveness in our society. This is reinforced because in their judgment of others, males are more influenced by attractiveness than females (item 182). In defining who is handicapped, females are more likely to include the unattractive (item 41). In a study of heterosexual attractiveness among college students, physically attractive students were liked more than unattractive students over a series of five dates (item 172).

In peer relations perceived physical attractiveness is related to social acceptance and friendship or sociometric selection (item 74). The strength of the variable of physical attractiveness over other factors, for example, ethnicity, has been documented (item 145).

As indicated in other sections of this essay, there appears to be a hierarchy of peer acceptance of the handicapped. Physical attractiveness is an element in this hierarchy which generally takes the form of preference for nonhandicapped over nonvisibly handicapped, and nonvisibly handicapped over visibly handicapped (item 236). Yet the more severely handicapped have probably not had the type of experiences that contribute to being socially skilled and to being able to manipulate others to like or be attracted to them. Research is needed to clarify the relationship between interpersonal skill, interpersonal evaluation, and physical appearance. The complexity of factors entering into the relationship between physical attractiveness and other variables is illustrated by findings such as that when raters were not acquainted with subjects, they rated the less attractive subjects as more likely to be antisocial in behavior, but that this was contradicted when subjects were known to the raters (item 282).

Reaction to physical attractiveness is not limited to youthful peer groups or social interpersonal situations. Even parents form expectations based upon this variable. Attractive children are assumed to be more successful than unattractive children on a number of measures of parental expectation (item 2). Probably the most important caretaker of children outside the home is the teacher. Research has shown that teachers succumb to the cultural stereotype and rate less attractive children as lower in intellectual ability (item 238). In addition to assuming higher intellectual functioning, teachers perceive the attractive child as more pleasing in personality and less likely to be a behavioral problem (item 230). Social scientists are well acquainted with the self-fulfilling prophecy. In this case children who are perceived as presenting potential behavior problems may well present such problems. There is some evidence to indicate that just as females are more at risk in terms of physical attractiveness in interpersonal situations, males are more at risk in school-authority situations (item 1).

The physical attractiveness of a child may be a factor in teachers' ratings more in early grades than in later grades, or only until the teacher gets to know the child more completely. Evidence suggests that classroom performance may alter initial expectations based on physical attractiveness (item 39). It is, of course, assumed that all children would be provided equal opportunity to perform or exhibit achievement. Research is needed to clarify differences between teachers' expectation ratings and actual classroom performance.

Few studies have explored the nature or source of factors that influence perception of physical attractiveness. There is some indication that attractiveness is perceived differently depending on the disability in question. For example, among patients with cleft palate, nasality is a factor in the perception of attractiveness (item 89). There is further evidence that these perceptions develop at specific ages and in specific situations (item 144).

The theory that physical disfigurement reduces attractiveness might be combined with other theories or stereotypes surrounding disability to produce explanatory breakthroughs and increase our understanding of a seemingly complicated phenomenon. For example, in one study the theory that handicap evokes sympathy was combined with the theory that disfigurement reduces attractiveness (item 247). Such a simple combination helped provide deeper insight into societal reaction to the handicapped. In that case, the more disfigured the individual, the less likely he was to receive help.

As a final comment on the state of knowledge relative to physical attractiveness, let us suggest that differences between attractive and unattractive subjects may be in the eye of the beholder, as some suggest (item 237) or they may be behavioral realities (item 144).

BEHAVIORAL FUNCTIONING OF THE DISABLED

For successful rehabilitation to take place, it is important to know the variables associated with return to optimal functioning. Optimal functioning is generally equated with relinquishment of the sick role. In permanent disabilities and in certain other conditions, this may be possible only in part or not at all.

Research has alerted us that sometimes the nature of the chronic disease or the reactions of significant others may impede medical efforts to maintain a patient at maximum levels of functioning. For example, in the early stages of chronic diseases, preferential treatment and associated protectiveness as well as socialization to the sick role may constitute such an impediment (item 116).

In some handicaps, manipulation of behavioral response is a possibility. For example, punishment and reward has been used to reduce blindisms such as eye poking, head rolling, and so on (item 17). It has been used with multiply handicapped blind students to teach mobility skills, to increase independent school seat work, and for other activities (item 83). The premise behind much of this modification is that the social integration of the handicapped will be facilitated if they can appear similar to normal, nondisabled individuals during contact.

One of the most frequently reported behavioral problems for the handicapped focuses on morale; in particular, feelings of depression and social isolation are frequent (items 15, 65, 136). In a study of morale following open-heart surgery, personality variables were reported to be as important as health perceptions in predicting morale (item 29). In some disabilities, particularly coronary heart disease, life dissatisfaction seems to be associated with severity of the condition (item 157). Among spinal-cord-injured patients, emotional reactions are related to the location of the injury (item 119). Clinicians need to be alert to these feelings and be able to intervene early in their development.

Many studies in the area of behavioral functioning focus on personality differences between specific patient groups and either siblings or normals. Research seems to be limited to certain well-defined groups, for example, those with cleft lip and/or palate, kidney transplants or patients on hemo-

with these two physical impairments engage in different personality adaptations. One response is that males with cleft lip and/or palate rate significantly higher on maturity and inhibition while orthopedically disabled males rate higher on aggression, activity level, and somatization.

An open question for research concerns the point at which terminally ill children become aware of their condition, and how they express anxiety and other feelings concerning it. Although they may not express their feelings directly, they do so indirectly through stories, fantasies, and so on (item 306).

Since people often turn to the supernatural when confronted with situations that are difficult to explain, do the disabled display a higher degree of religiosity than the normal population? Little empirical evidence exists on this subject. One study of heart patients investigated the role of religion in providing support to individuals recovering from life-threatening situations (item 48). The study found that the heart attack did not alter religious or secular attitudes, nor did it lead to increased dependency on religious institutions or clergy. No significant changes in level of religiosity, patterns of church attendance, or in secular orientations to life and illness experience were noted over the first year.

In this section on the behavioral functioning of the handicapped we have noted some differences between specific disabled groups and comparison groups of siblings or individuals drawn from nonhandicapped populations. Evidence seems clear that most findings hold true for only one specific handicapped group and cannot be generalized across categories or classes. Also, the problems treated have mainly concerned broad psychological and social differences. There is a need for more in-depth study that addresses dimensions of these broader problems.

ACADEMIC AND INTELLECTUAL FUNCTIONING

One topical area on which there is an abundance of accumulated research knowledge concerns academic or classroom performance and intellectual functioning. Studies on patient groups with various disabilities report no differences between specific groups of handicapped and nonhandicapped or siblings in educational achievement. Among epileptic groups studied neither frequency nor type of seizure was correlated with academic achievement (item 105). Similar findings were noted for the orthopedically disabled, among whom type of

dialysis, the blind, the hearing impaired, epileptics, and spina bifida children. It is difficult, if not impossible, to generalize to all categories of disabled or handicapped. Often no differences are noted between the groups being compared, but as more variables are added to the analysis or to the regression equation, differences do appear.

Strong evidence does not exist to suggest that specific forms of somatic disability are associated with particular personality problems, or that extent of psychological effects of disability are proportional to severity of the disability.

In studying personality manifestations in physically handicapped individuals, researchers should bear in mind that personality is a complicated mechanism affected by many variables. Physical disability may be only one of these variables. This conclusion is verified in the results of a study which found no significant differences in self-concept among paraplegics, hospitalized tuberculosis patients, and a nonhospitalized control group (item 204). Handicap does not operate in a vacuum; other factors that may contribute to emotional or behavioral disturbances among the handicapped include increased biological vulnerability and psychosocial hazards such as family disturbances (item 261). For example, psychiatric disorders are twice as common among handicapped children when their physical condition also involves disease or damage of the brain (item 261). This illustrates the cumulative effect associated with the presence of more than one physical disability plus social or psychological problems.

Earlier in this section reference was made to depression and morale problems among kidney patients. Apparently such problems develop over time. A study of children treated for kidney transplantation found no clearcut personality differences between this group and a comparison group of children (item 139). However, another study that involved different age groups found that renal dialysis patients exhibit a fear of death and a sense of hopelessness. The patients who were older, and had been on dialysis longest, manifested the greatest sense of personal distress (item 31).

A number of studies have been conducted on patients with cleft lip and/or palate. No specific personality type is associated with this disability (item 319), nor does this group exhibit a higher number of serious psychiatric problems or conflicts than controls (item 270).

Some traits, however, have been reported consistently by other researchers. Preschool children with oral-facial clefts were found to be more passive than a noncleft group (item 277) and less physically aggressive as teenagers (item 275); they were rated by teachers as displaying more inhibition of impulses (item 237) and were viewed by their mothers as more dependent than control siblings (item 270). In a series of studies on social functioning of adults, this patient group scored significantly lower than siblings and randomly selected controls in regard to geographic mobility, initiating social contacts, and membership in voluntary associations (item 217). In terms of extracurricular participation in high school, members of this group were labeled as observers rather than participants (item 299).

Among epileptics, type of seizure is not correlated with negative social development (items 105, 188), but frequency of seizure has negative effects (item 105). Epileptic college students differed from controls on MMPI profiles (item 188). The fact of unpredictability of seizure and inability to anticipate how others will react to them might contribute to some of the differences between those with and those without epilepsy. It would be of interest to compare epileptics to groups with other types of seizures such as persons who suffer from spells of diabetic coma or shock.

Cultural expectations are important in determining whether a handicap will contribute to personality or behavioral problems. For example, the emphasis on physical beauty, particularly for females, may contribute to personality differences noted for college-age females with severe acne (item 325), and emphasis on occupational achievement of males may contribute to their more negative reaction to stuttering, a condition that can limit employment opportunities (item 269).

One behavioral variable that has received serious research scrutiny is aggression. Men and boys who exhibit what is commonly labeled as Type A behavior, that is, high levels of aggressiveness and competition, seek to exert control over uncontrollable events. These individuals have higher rates of coronary heart disease than Type B individuals, who are less competitive and aggressive. What is striking, however, is that the basis for adult heart attacks may already be present in childhood behavior patterns (item 173). This poses challenges for clinical intervention.

Evidence suggests that unattractive children aggress against peers more often than attractive children do, and that this aggression is a behavioral reality, not just something imagined by significant others (item 144). In a study of children with minor physical deviations such as widely spaced eyes, it was found that subjects with these conditions scored higher on measures of problem behavior than children without such problems (item 102). In this study, high scores on problem behavior were negatively associated with friendship among boys. Thus, there seems to be a compounding of problems of social functioning for the unattractive.

There is strong evidence to suggest that disability is related to locus of control, i.e., to the degree to which an individual perceives life events to be a consequence of his or her behavior. Persons high on external locus of control feel that events are beyond their control and depend largely on factors outside themselves such as environmental, familial, or social factors. Persons high on internal control perceive themselves as the primary architects of their own life course. Children with clefts were found to be significantly more external in control, and mothers who were more external in control had children who were more field dependent and more external in control (item 27). A study of young adult deaf students found that they scored higher on external control than normal hearing students (item 21). This study also linked locus of control to parentage, but suggested that the child's deafness coupled with lack of verbal stimulation between parent and child resulted in external control orientation. The early period of disability may be the more important in determining locus of control since it is marked by expectations of increased direction from external forces (item 315). Factors shown to be not related to locus of control include being institutionalized (item 315) and degree of mobility among the orthopedically disabled (item 123).

One important developmental area concerns sexuality and relationships to the opposite sex. In a study that compared college students who depended on wheelchairs for mobility to a random control group of students, no differences were found between the two groups relative to attitudes toward and feelings about sexual behavior. The disabled group did score significantly lower in relation to feelings about their own sexuality than did the nondisabled group (item 73).

Studies of adult subjects with cleft lip and/or palate note a higher rate of singleness than among siblings and comparison controls (items 185, 214). The latter study also noted a higher degree of childlessness and later age at marriage. Females with cleft lip conditions seem to be particularly vulnerable, that is, the differences between females with clefts and their counterparts without clefts are greater than they are between the male groups.

Those studies that report on more than one type of disability can be particularly helpful in contributing to our theoretical knowledge. They allow us to compare disability states and also to determine whether generalizations can be made across disability states. For example, one study compared personality characteristics of children with cleft lip and/or palate to a group of children with orthopedic disabilities (item 240). The results indicated that individuals disability and degree of mobility did not correlate with school achievement (item 123). For subjects with cleft lip and/or palate there were no differences between cleft type and educational achievement (item 185), but the latter study did report differences in educational aspirations.

Negative academic outcomes are reported in some studies. The negatives include: academic ratings of children with clefts (item 27), delayed achievement for hearing-impaired children (item 56), and reading and communication problems for language-impaired children (item 101).

Clinical intervention may be called for in some cases. For example, hearing-impaired children from more secure homes made significantly better progress than children from families with emotional problems (item 168), and self-concept was found to differentiate between blind college students who persisted through the freshman year and those who dropped out (item 271).

In the previous section on behavioral functioning, reference was made to the teacher's perceptions of higher inhibition in children with cleft lip and/or palate (item 239). Another study that dealt with the same disability group suggested that it is the number, not the kind, of handicap that influences behavioral performance in school (item 82). This again suggests that disability has a cumulative effect and that individuals with more than one disabling condition have heightened problems.

Scores on intellectual functioning appear to be influenced by the nature of the disability. Some studies noted no difference in intelligence for deaf as compared to normal hearing children (item 135), and in fact, the hearing-impaired scored higher than normals on some dimensions, for example, fluency and originality (item 125) and creative thinking (item 121). These findings shed light on the nature of intellectual functioning in the absence of language.

Research also indicates that epileptic seizures have no effect on children's intelligence (item 107). However, age at onset (early age) is a factor in impairment of adult mental ability (item 62) and increased frequency of major motor seizures is associated with impaired cognitive functioning in adults.

The evidence is different for subjects with cleft lip and/or palate. Children and teenagers with clefts score lower on IQ tests than their siblings (item 156). This suggests that perhaps the condition or factors associated with it and not inherited characteristics may contribute to a patient's IQ. However, IQ tests generally have several dimensions. One study indicates that the deficiencies noted among clefts are expressive, not cognitive (item 68). Just as they are most vulnerable in terms of facial attractiveness and some aspects of social functioning, females with cleft lip and palate may be the most vulnerable subgroup of the cleft population in terms of intellectual functioning. They scored lower on certain subtests than any other cleft subgroup (item 142). Apparently differences in intellectual development between cleft and normal subjects can be identified early, even in children below three years of age (item 77). This evidence argues for early intervention to prevent developmental delays from becoming greater with time.

Research on instructional goals of handicapped as compared to nonhandicapped university students indicates that handicapped students are more cognitively inclined (item 151). The researchers indicate that this may be a result of higher availability of time to develop cognitive skills.

Institutionalization has negative consequences for social interaction patterns of hard of hearing children. These consequences are apparent when the children are compared to normals and the hearing impaired in normal school settings (item 163). Integrated settings for blind children facilitate the social interaction of that group with their sighted peers, and promote social maturity and independence, without sacrificing necessary Braille skills (item 181).

After many years' existence of a separate educational system for the hearing impaired, many unanswered questions remain as to how learning takes place among this group (item 44) and the effectiveness of various instructional modes (item 45).

CONCLUSIONS

The content reported in the various sections of this review essay indicates that we are able to make some very broad generalizations about social and behavioral research on the physically handicapped. For example, we have agreement on the way in which society perceives and ranks different types of disability; we have indications that a strong self-concept aids in acceptance of disability, in chances for vocational success, and in a number of other ways. We also have knowledge about the relation or association of some specific variables with behaviors, attitudes, social functioning, and so on. These research findings can guide practitioners in their work with clients.

However, much of this knowledge is limited to a specific handicapped type. Contradictions occur when we compare across disability types. Clinicians must be aware of these discrepancies and exercise caution when using research findings in their work. At the same time, researchers must improve their level of methodological sophistication and increase the scope and complexity of their endeavors.

THE STUDIES

1. Adams, Gerald R. "Racial Membership and Physical Attractiveness Effects on Pre-School Teachers' Expectations." *Child Study Journal*, 8, 1 (Winter 1978): 29-41.

    240 preschool teachers in a Head Start and Early Intervention project were interviewed to assess the effects of racial membership, sex, and physical attractiveness on initial expectations. The subjects were shown photographs which they rated on the degree of facial attractiveness (Likert Scale and Q Sort were used). The stimulus (index child) was rated on his or her intellectual achievement, classroom behavior, social behavior, and athletic ability. Unattractive boys and black youths were given less favorable ratings on the dependent measures.

2. Adams, Gerald R., and LaVoie, Joseph C. "Parental Expectations of Educational and Personal-Social Performance and Child-Rearing Patterns as a Function of Attractiveness, Sex and Conduct of the Child." *Child Study Journal*, 5, 3 (Summer 1975): 125-142.

    197 middle-class parents of elementary school children were asked to read a student progress report for a child whose conduct rating was good or poor. Attached to the report was a color photograph of a child who had previously been judged to be of a higher or lower physical attractiveness. After reading the student progress report, parents made a number of ratings. Findings were as follows:
    (1) There was a positive relationship between good conduct and high academic performance.
    (2) There was no relationship between physical attractiveness and academic performance.
    (3) Attractive children were assumed to acquire higher status jobs.
    (4) Attractive children were rated more popular, more likely to be elected to class office, and as having

more positive personal attitudes than less attractive children.
(5) Sex discrimination still exists among parents regarding what is appropriate and inappropriate for boys and girls.
(6) Of the three variables, the one most influencing parental ratings was the child's conduct.

3. Albrecht, Gary L., and Higgins, Paul C. "Rehabilitation Success: The Interrelationship of Multiple Criteria." *Journal of Health and Social Behavior*, 18 (March 1977): 36-45.

This article reviews various measures of rehabilitation success to ascertain the interrelationship of functioning on the various "success" criteria. The criteria are based on a review of the rehabilitation literature as well as observation and interviews in rehabilitation settings. Data on 122 patients in two rehabilitation settings, one public and one private, are presented. Indicators of success are divided into physical and social functioning. The multiple indicators of physical functioning correlate quite highly, are moderately related to assessments of social functioning, and are less related to self-administered indicators of social functioning. The study also contributes the following: there was little difference in the results of care between the public and private setting, the staff judgment of cooperation and completion of service was not related to improvement in physical functioning. Results lead to questioning of the traditional "sick role" model.

4. Almajor, Moshe; Jaffe, Yoram; and Lomranz, Jacob. "The Relation Between Limb Dominance, Acceptance of Disability and the Phantom-Limb Phenomenon." *Journal of Abnormal Psychology*, 87, 3 (June 1978): 377-379.

18 double-amputees who had lost two homologous-limbs while in military service responded to questionnaires about limb dominance, acceptance of disability, and frequency of phantom-limb sensation (PLS). The findings showed a positive association between limb dominance and PLS, but no association between acceptance of disability and PLS. The authors conclude the presence of PLS is related to physiological rather than psychological factors.

5. Anderson, Elizabeth M., and Plewis, Ian. "Impairment of a Motor Skill in Children with Spina Bifida Cystica

and Hydrocephalus: An Exploratory Study." *British Journal of Psychology*, 68, 1 (February 1977): 61-70.

Next to cerebral palsy, spina bifida is responsible for the largest group of physically handicapped children in Britain. This study reports on two experiments comparing spina bifida children to normals. Motor tasks were involved in each case. In both instances, the spina bifida children exhibited impairment, but with practice their performance improved. The authors stress the importance of repeated practice at motor tasks for this group.

6. Asher, Nancy Weinberg. "Manipulating Attraction Toward the Disabled: An Application of the Similarity-Attraction Model." *Rehabilitation Psychology*, 20, 4 (Winter 1973): 156-164.

Tests the hypothesis that when a disabled person is perceived as attitudinally similar to a nondisabled person, his or her attractiveness increases. Groups rated were attitudinally similar and dissimilar and able-bodied and disabled. Similarity increased the attraction of both the able-bodied and the disabled. There were no differences between the able-bodied and the disabled ratings in the two groups of attitude similarity and dissimilarity.

7. Ayer, M. Jane. "Employability of Handicapped Individuals in the Teaching Professions: Considerations for Rehabilitation Counseling." *Rehabilitation Counseling Bulletin*, 13, 4 (June 1970): 364-373.

322 school administrators completed a questionnaire assessing whether individuals with physical and emotional disabilities were perceived as employable as teachers. Findings were as follows:
  (1) Younger administrators were more willing to hire handicapped individuals than older administrators.
  (2) There was greater willingness to hire those individuals with controlled seizures than those with uncontrolled (neurological impairment) in both groups.
  (3) Facial disfigurement was viewed as unemployable condition, with older school administrators less willing to hire them.

8. Bachman, Winnie H. "Variables Affecting Post-School Economic Adaptation of Orthopedically Handicapped and

Other Health-Impaired Students." *Rehabilitation Literature*, 33, 4 (April 1972): 98-102, 114.

A structured interview was conducted with 167 subjects between the ages of 18 and 26 who attended public special education classes. Of the 167 subjects, 89 were still in school, 27 were employed, and 51 were unemployed. Variables found to be associated with employment were completion of high school, work experiences in school, and good hand use and mobility. Placement of students with nonhandicapped classmates was *not* related to effective employment.

9. Baker, Larry D., and Reitz, H. Joseph. "Altruism Toward the Blind: Effects of Sex of Helper and Dependency of Victim." *Journal of Social Psychology*, 104, 1 (February 1978): 19-28.

This study reports on a field experiment designed to explore the social environment of the blind with emphasis on societal reaction to dependency. The central question is whether blind persons would be helped more than sighted persons in situations in which sight is not essential to problem resolution. A caller sought help from 428 adults randomly selected from a telephone directory. The caller identified self as either blind or sighted, and constructed a situation of high or low dependency. The blind caller received help more often than the sighted, as did the caller in the high dependency situation. Females responded more sensitively to both vision and situational dependency than males did. The research raises the question of how society responds to the handicap of blindness and what the response means for self-image of the blind.

10. Beene, Gary M., and Larson, Janet. "Misdiagnosis in Rehabilitation Settings with the Hearing Impaired Client." *Journal of Rehabilitation of the Deaf*, 13, 2 (October 1979): 11-14.

This study investigates the frequency of misdiagnosis of hearing-impaired clients in rehabilitation and counseling settings. The focus is on agreement with original assessment of clients on agency intake forms. Seven counselors in six settings reevaluated five of their hearing-impaired clients' files at random. They sought to determine if the client was functioning at a higher or lower level than originally assessed. The mean level of reevaluation agreement with the original diagnosis was 65.7% with a range of 40% agreement by two counselors to 100% agreement by one counselor. 22.8% of original assessments were reevaluated as too high and 11.4% were reevaluated as too low.

11. Bentivegna, Joseph, and Newman, Joseph. "Rehabilitation Problems Among 'Black Lung' Miners." *Journal of Rehabilitation*, 44, 2 (April-June 1978): 19-21, 36.

This study reports survey data that compares "black lung" and non-"black lung" miners on various aspects of rehabilitation such as perception of seriousness of disease, number and types of other disabilities, attitude toward vocational rehabilitation, and overall rehabilitation experiences. "Black lung" miners are viewed as having rehabilitation problems comparable to those of other handicapped persons with similar severity of disability and similar circumstances. Generally, the disabled miner viewed vocational rehabilitation as impractical. This view was associated with severe respiratory disease, advanced middle age, limited education and work background, rural residence and unwillingness to physically relocate.

12. Benton, R.B.; Permenter, N.A.; Baylor, J.; and McLelland, P. "Evaluating the Work Potential of Blind Multiply Handicapped Persons for the Manufacture of Bath Perfume." *New Outlook for the Blind*, 68, 1 (January 1974): 20-24.

A project to evaluate the ability of blind persons to become engaged in the manufacture of bath perfume was mounted within already existing industry. The success rate was 83%. An interesting finding was the high level of performance of the blind relative to the low expectation for their work by factory staff.

13. Bentzen, Billie Louise. "Production and Testing of an Orientation and Travel Map for Visually Handicapped Persons." *New Outlook for the Blind*, 66, 8 (October 1972): 249-255.

This study tests the hypothesis that a tactual map facilitates independent travel skills by the blind in unfamiliar areas. The map served as the only source of information on the area. Subjects in the study experienced no difficulty in planning travel routes. Variations were reported in terms of individual handling of the map. Trials were conducted on blind persons with various demographic and sight characteristics.

14. Ben-Yishay, Yehuda; Gerstman, Louis; Diller, Leonard; and Haas, Albert. "Prediction of Rehabilitation Outcomes from Psychometric Parameters in Left Hemiplegics." *Journal of Consulting and Clinical Psychology*, 34, 3 (June 1970): 436-441.

Both a full and partial battery of psychometric predictors were used with subjects who had suffered strokes and were rendered left hemiplegics. Prediction of outcome of rehabilitation was possible from use of the psychometric predictors upon initiation of rehabilitation. Thus, it may be possible to screen patients for success at the outset of a rehabilitation program.

15. Bernstein, Dorothy M. "After Transplantation--The Child's Emotional Reactions." *American Journal of Psychiatry*, 127, 9 (March 1971): 1189-1193.

This is a report on a longitudinal study focused on the emotional reactions of children who received renal transplants. The period covered is from discharge to six years later. Significant emotional reactions occurred in 4 of 32 children. Case material is provided. The need for alertness to identify emotional problems in children who have undergone renal transplants is stressed.

16. Bilodeau, Carolyn Bascom, and Hackett, Thomas P. "Issues Raised in Group Setting by Patients Recovering from Myocardial Infarction." *American Journal of Psychiatry*, 128, 1 (July 1971): 73-78.

Convalescent male heart patients met in a group setting for twelve weeks. Concerns centered on group process, current and future states of health, effects of illness on aspects of life, their role in the family, history of their illness, and medical care after discharge. The group meetings were viewed by patients as an aid both in accepting illness and in adjustment.

17. Blasch, Bruce B. "Blindisms: Treatment by Punishment and Reward in Laboratory and Natural Settings." *Journal of Visual Impairment and Blindness*, 72, 6 (June 1978): 215-230.

The results of six independent experiments to test the effectiveness of using punishment and positive reinforcers to reduce blindisms are reported. Blindisms are stereotypic behavior. Blindisms measured in this report include head-rolling, rocking of head and trunk, and eye-poking. Data indicated a marked decrease in the blindisms. Also, symptom substitutions, i.e., moving from one blindism to another, did not occur. Symptom reduction generalized to other classroom or nonexperimental situations, and other types of behavioral symptoms also disappeared.

18. Blood, Gordon W., and Hyman, Melvin. "Children's Perception of Nasal Resonance." *Journal of Speech and Hearing Disorders*, 42, 3 (August 1977): 446-448.

    The purpose of this study was to investigate children's perception of nasal resonance in other children. A total of 120 elementary-school-aged children listened to four female voices with from normal resonance to severe hypernasality. They responded to a total of 20 questions such as: Did you like the person telling the story? The findings indicated that the children responded negatively, as early as kindergarten, to severe hypernasality. The findings suggest that hypernasality is a disorder that warrants treatment.

19. Bloombaum, Milton, and Gugelyk, Ted. "Voluntary Confinement Among Lepers." *Journal of Health and Social Behavior*, 11, 1 (March 1970): 16-20.

    This is a study of a leper colony, Kalaupapa, Hawaii. The purpose is to explore why patients in whom the disease has been arrested through sulfones elect to remain in confinement when eligible to return to their communities. The stigma of leprosy in the form of physical disfigurement and the effects of prolonged tenure in the colony are held most probably to account for this form of reverse isolation.

20. Bobath, Berta, and Finnie, Nancie R. "Problems of Communication between Parents and Staff in the Treatment and Management of Children with Cerebral Palsy." *Developmental Medicine and Child Neurology*, 12, 5 (October 1970): 629-635.

    Parental cooperation is important in the treatment and management of children with cerebral palsy. This study presents questionnaire findings from a survey of 40 parents of children with cerebral palsy who were clients of the Western Cerebral Palsy Centre in London. Findings include: technical terms should be avoided when explaining the child's condition and prognosis to parents; parents should be given clear statements on how treatment and everyday activities link; surveys give parents an opportunity to indicate frustrations that they cannot express verbally; domestic situations must be considered when prescribing treatment.

21. Bodner, Barbara A., and Johns, Jeannie. "Personality and Hearing Impairment: A Study in Locus of Control." *Volta Review*, 79 (October-November 1977): 362-372.

   228 child and adult deaf students were studied in relation to locus of control, which refers to the degree to which an individual perceives events in his/her life as being a consequence of his/her own behavior. The findings indicate that the deaf students scored significantly higher on external control than did normal hearing students. The authors interpret the findings to support the idea that the child's deafness, coupled with the lack of verbal stimulation between parent and child, results in the external control orientation.

22. Bolton, Brian. "A Behavior-Oriented Treatment Program for Deaf Clients Comprehensive Rehabilitation Center." *American Journal of Orthopsychiatry*, 44, 3 (April 1974): 376-385.

   180 multiple-handicapped deaf adults were the subjects of this study. They were severely limited in the ability to communicate, emotionally immature, vocationally unprepared, and functionally illiterate. A behavior-oriented program focusing on personal-social preparatory services as well as vocational preparatory services was employed. Findings indicated that half of the clients served were placed in competitive employment. Deaf clients with previous work experiences who completed training were more likely to achieve competitive employment.

23. Bolton, Brian. "Factors Contributing to Successful Rehabilitation of Deaf Clients." *Journal of Rehabilitation of the Deaf*, 9, 2 (October 1975): 36-43.

   This report presents the results of statistical analysis of biographic, psychometric, and social parameter client data and rehabilitation outcomes for three samples of deaf clients. The purpose is to determine which combination of predictor variables explains the variability of client outcomes. Two conclusions are: predictability improves as more information about the client is included in the regression equation, and predictors of employment for deaf rehabilitation clients are specific to the service program and client population.

24. Bolton, Brian. "Dimensions of Client Change: Replication." *Rehabilitation Counseling Bulletin*, 22, 1 (September 1978): 8-14.

The purpose of this study was to assess what factors are associated with client change during rehabilitation. The sample consisted of 31 clients who were served by eight counselors in the Little Rock office of the Arkansas Rehabilitative Service. Each client completed the Human Service Scale and was evaluated by his counselor who completed the Client Outcome Measure (at the time of acceptance for services and again at closure). The findings revealed a positive correlation between economic-vocational variables and the client's self-reported improvement in emotional security. Improvement in the economic-vocational area is related to, and therefore may be facilitated by, improvement in self-perceived emotional adjustment. The broadest conclusion supportable at the present time is that psychosocial adjustment and vocational adjustment are distinguishable yet related dimensions of client improvement during the rehabilitation counseling process.

25. Bolton, Brian, and Sommer, Patricia. "Mode of Address and Patient Satisfaction in Rehabilitation: An Experimental Study." *Journal of Health and Social Behavior*, 11, 3 (September 1970): 215-219.

In this study 20 physically handicapped adult patients were randomly assigned to reciprocal formal and reciprocal informal address conditions for an experimental period of eight weeks. A scale was devised to measure patient satisfaction with the occupational and physical therapies they received. Attitudes of patients and staff toward experimental conditions were assessed through interviews. Patients more often preferred the informal, and professionals the formal manner of address. It was concluded that reciprocal informal address may be an easy way of democratizing the professional patient relationship, thus giving patients a feeling of more active participation in their rehabilitation.

26. Bonfanti, Barbara. "Effects of Training on Nonverbal and Verbal Behaviors of Congenitally Blind Adults."

Journal of Visual Impairment and Blindness, 73, 1 (January 1979): 1-9.

This study is based on the premise that social interaction of blind people will be facilitated if they can appear similar to sighted individuals during contact. The study utilized behavior inventories on congenitally and adventitiously blind subjects. The findings indicate that blind individuals can be trained to modify both nonverbal (blindisms) behavior and verbal behavior. The training program is summarized.

27. Brantley, Helen T., and Clifford, Edward. "Maternal and Child Locus of Control and Field-Dependence in Cleft Palate Children." *Cleft Palate Journal*, 16, 2 (April 1979): 183-187.

44 cleft palate children, 9 to 18 years of age, and their mothers were compared to 61 control children and their mothers. Maternal variables included locus of control and perceived reactions to the child's birth. Child variables included locus of control, field dependence, parental perceptions, and teacher ratings. Mothers of children with cleft palates indicated a significantly greater negative impact at their children's births but did not indicate greater externality. Children with clefts were significantly more external in control, were more field-dependent, perceived parental reactions as more negative, and had more negative academic ratings. Mothers who were external in locus of control had children who were more field-dependent and had more external control.

28. Brown, Julia S., and Rawlinson, May. "Relinquishing the Sick Role Following Open-Heart Surgery." *Journal of Health and Social Behavior*, 16, 1 (March 1975): 12-27.

155 persons were administered a semantic differential scale to measure the distance between self and sick person one year plus after open-heart surgery. A regression analysis was employed.

It was clear that persons who successfully survived open-heart surgery regarded sick persons less favorably than they regarded people generally. These individuals judged themselves to be, both before and after surgery, more independent, better, and more active than other sick persons. Five factors were particularly important in determining the tendency of the patient to relinquish the sick role after surgery.

In order of explanatory power these were: depression (less depressed), preoperative tendency to reject sick role, duration of illness prior to surgery (short), age (youth), and sex (male). For successful rehabilitation, it is important to know the variables that are associated with returning to optimal functioning.

29. Brown, Julia S., and Rawlinson, May. "The Morale of Patients Following Open-Heart Surgery." *Journal of Health and Social Behavior*, 17, 2 (June 1976): 134-144.

Interview data was obtained from 150 patients one year or more following open-heart surgery. Multiple regression analysis was utilized to assess the relative influence of 11 medical, psychological, social, and demographic variables on the patient's morale. Males and females differed in terms of the predictive variables associated with morale. For males the best predictors of higher morale were lack of proneness to depression, length of illness (shorter time, better morale), tendency to be repressor rather than a sensitizer in coping style, married rather than single, and view of self as not currently enacting sick role. For women, the most apparent manifestation of morale was associated with not reporting many physical symptoms. Overall, personality variables were reported as commensurate in importance with health perceptions as predictors of morale. This has import for future studies of morale among other groups of chronically ill, disabled, or handicapped.

30. Bruininks, Virginia L. "Actual and Perceived Peer Status of Learning-Disabled Students in Mainstream Programs." *Journal of Special Education*, 12 (1978): 51-58.

A study was undertaken of 16 learning-disabled students matched for age and grade with 16 non-learning-disabled students. Both groups of students completed the Peer Acceptance Scale. The results showed that the learning-disabled students were less socially accepted than their classmates in regular classrooms. The author argues that a focus of educational remediation must be the learning-disabled student's perception of self and others.

31. Burke, Henry R. "Renal Patients and their MMPI Profiles," *Journal of Psychology*, 101, 2 (March 1979): 229-235.

Three groups of patients on renal dialysis were compared with one another, with a group of predialysis patients, and with a general medical population. Findings confirmed earlier research that dialysis patients would exhibit fear of death and a sense of helplessness. The group manifesting the greatest sense of personal distress was composed of the oldest, most variable patients who were also on dialysis the longest time.

32. Byrd, E. Keith; Byrd, Dianne; and Emener, William G. "Student, Counselor and Employer Perceptions of Employability of Severely Retarded." *Rehabilitation Literature*, 38, 2 (February 1977): 42-44.

27 disabilities were presented to students, counselors, and employers in the Tallahassee, Florida, area to assess employability of each handicapped group. The primary finding was that the employers and counselor ratings were similar and differed from those of the students. For example, alcoholics were ranked as least employable by the counselors and employees but not by the students. The findings raise questions about the need for continuing education for the counselors.

33. Casella, Lucinda C. "The Deaf Job Seeker and Employment Agencies." *Journal of Rehabilitation of the Deaf*, 11, 3 (January 1978): 23-25.

This study reports on a survey to assess utilization of employment agencies by the deaf. It seeks to determine: (a) the total number of deaf people who have applied for jobs through employment agencies, (b) what types of jobs were found, and (c) the mode of communication used by the deaf job seeker. The data indicates that only a small number of deaf individuals seek jobs through employment agencies; blue collar agencies are utilized most often; communication was dependent on written messages and speech-reading.

34. Chaiklin, Harris, and Warfield, Martha. "Stigma Management and Amputee Rehabilitation." *Rehabilitation Literature*, 34, 6 (June 1973): 162-166.

This study tested the hypothesis that there is a relationship between modes of stigma management and progress toward rehabilitation goals. Subjects were 24 patients of the Department of Physical Medicine and Rehabilitation at the University of Maryland during the months of February, March, and April 1970. The findings indicated that those patients who tended to deny stigma made less adequate progress in their treatment. The findings support the premise that denial is an ineffective coping strategy for the handicapped individual.

35. Chapman, James W., and Boersma, Fredrick J. "Learning Disabilities, Locus of Control and Mother's Attitudes." *Journal of Educational Psychology*, 71 (1979): 250-258.

   Locus of control and mothers' attitudes concerning school performance were studied in 81 learning-disabled and 81 normally achieving children, in grades three to six. Learning-disabled children indicated more external perception of control with respect to successful academic performance. Mothers of learning-disabled children reported more negative and fewer positive expectations for their children. The importance of mothers' attitudes for school learning was discussed.

36. Christie, David, and Lawrence, Lorraine. "Patients and Hospitals: A Study of the Attitudes of Stroke Patients." *Social Science and Medicine*, 12, 1A (January 1978): 49-51.

   60 survivors of a cerebrovascular accident were interviewed at approximately six months after the acute episode. The patients' attitudes towards the teaching hospital in which they received initial care were assessed. These attitudes were not associated with social class, residual disability, or length of stay, but were strongly related to age and sex. With increasing age men regarded the hospital environment less favorably, with changing attitudes towards doctors a major factor. In the case of women this trend was reversed, and more positive attitudes were associated with increasing age. 12 non-English speaking subjects viewed their hospital experience less favorably than the others. The technical skills of medical staff were highly regarded by most patients. However, the ability of medical staff to communicate and relate to stroke patients often was thought to be inadequate.

37. Cimperman, A., and Dunn, Michael. "Group Therapy with Spinal Cord Injured Patients: A Case Study." *Rehabilitation Psychology*, 21, 1 (Spring 1974): 44-48.

   This article reports on the application of group therapy techniques with spinal cord injury patients. The group was informal, did not require attendance, and emphasized current concerns of the group members. Emphasis in this report is on techniques to use with spinal-cord-injured patients, particularly as related to group structuring and expectations of both group leader and group members. Topics reported as important to the group were: plans for the future, reactions of others to disability, sex, and suicide.

38. Clifford, Edward, and Crocker, Eleanor C. "Maternal Responses: The Birth of a Normal Child as Compared to the Birth of a Child with a Cleft." *Cleft Palate Journal*, 8, 3 (July 1971): 298-306.

100 mothers of normal babies and 75 mothers of babies with cleft lip and/or palate were interviewed when their children were approximately six months old. The findings were as follows:
(1) There was no difference in marital satisfaction.
(2) There was no difference in sexual adjustment.
(3) Mothers of babies with cleft lip and/or palate responded with shock, and the degree of shock was related to delay in showing the baby to the mother in the hospital.

39. Clifford, Margaret M. "Physical Attractiveness and Academic Performance." *Child Study Journal*, 5, 4 (Fall 1975): 201-210.

Two studies were conducted to investigate the relationship between physical attractiveness and academic performance. In the first study a fully scored first grade report card with an attached photo was used to elicit teacher expectations. It was found that teachers expressed more favorable academic ratings for attractive students than for unattractive students. The second study examined correlations between attractiveness ratings and several achievement ratings for second, fourth, and sixth grade students. No significant linear function was evidenced in this study. Findings raise questions as to whether there are differences between expectation ratings and actual class performance. The latter may alter initial expectations based on physical attractiveness.

40. Coet, Larry J. "Defining the Term, 'Handicap': a Function of Sex, Race, Religion, and Geographic Location." *Psychological Reports*, 41 (1977): 783-787.

100 subjects characterized by sex, race (Caucasian-Mexican American), religion (affiliation-no affiliation), and geographical location (urban-rural) were given a

questionnaire asking them to rank five groups of individuals they considered handicapped. Findings were as follows:
  (1) Males emphasized "lack of education as a handicap," while females stressed "deafness" and "birth defects."
  (2) Mexican Americans listed "minority" more frequently as a handicap, whereas Caucasian subjects placed more emphasis on "deafness" and "physical injury."
  (3) No significant differences were found in relation to religion and geographic location.

41. Coet, Larry J., and Thornton, Larry W. "Age and Sex: Factors in Defining the Term 'Handicap.'" *Psychological Reports*, 37 (1975): 103-106.

A random sample of 67 males and 74 females were divided into three age groups: 12 to 25, 26 to 45, and 46 to 82 years old. Subjects were given a questionnaire asking them to rank five groups of people they felt should be labeled "handicapped." Results indicated that the definitions differed according to age and sex. Males emphasized "social" and "intellectual" conditions as handicaps while females stressed the more visible (physically unattractive) conditions. The youngest age group listed "race," "speech," and "socio-economic" conditions as handicaps more frequently, while the middle-aged group was more concerned with "physical incapacitation," "blindness," and "heart disease." The oldest group stressed "mental illness" and "mental retardation" most frequently.

42. Cohen, Shirley. "Teacher Receptivity to the Concept of Parent Participation in the Education of Handicapped Children: Some Preliminary Findings." *Rehabilitation Literature*, 38, 5 (March 1977): 151-153.

41 educators from service programs for handicapped children completed a questionnaire assessing parents' participation in the education of their handicapped children. Ten of the 12 possible items of parent participation received strong support by the teachers. No differences were noted when parents were teaching assistants in classrooms with their children, or when parents were rejected as teaching assistants in the same classes as their children.

43. Columbus, Dorothy, and Fogel, Max L. "Survey of Disabled Persons Reveal Housing Choices." *Journal of Rehabilitation*, 37, 2 (March-April 1971): 26-28.

    A survey of 371 patients at several Philadelphia-based rehabilitation centers was undertaken to assess housing preferences. Segregated facilities for physically disabled were rejected when age, sex, and level of employment were analyzed. The only difference was that non-visual disabilities (e.g., cardiovascular) rejected segregated housing significantly more often than visible disabilities such as orthopedic cases.

44. Conrad, R. "Short-Term Memory Processes in the Deaf." *British Journal of Psychology*, 61, 2 (May 1970): 179-195.

    This is a report on two experiments using deaf subjects. The purpose is to answer the question of how the deaf memorize. The answer has implications for education of the deaf. The results show that there is no overall pattern followed by all subjects. Rather, different individual use different strategies, or several strategies may be utilized by one individual. The study confirms learning and thinking processes in a group without speech. It leaves open the question of how these processes take place.

45. Conrad, R. "The Effect of Vocalizing on Comprehension in the Profoundly Deaf." *British Journal of Psychology*, 62, 2 (May 1971): 147-150.

    Hearing and profoundly deaf children were tested for comprehension after reading prose passages either silently or aloud. Some of the deaf relied primarily on articulatory coding to memorize verbal material while others relied more on visual code. The visual reliance group comprehended much less when they read aloud than when they read silently. The two deaf groups performed equally well after silent reading. After reading aloud, the comprehension difference was significant. Reading mode showed no effect between the hearing controls and the deaf. The results pose questions for instruction of the deaf.

46. Cook, Daniel W.; Kunce, Joseph T.; and Getsinger, Stephen H. "Perceptions of the Disabled and Counseling Effectiveness." *Rehabilitation Counseling Bulletin*, 19, 3 (March 1976): 470-475.

This study investigated differences in counselors' perceptions of disabled and nondisabled persons, taking into account the sex of the counselors and their judged effectiveness. 80 personnel assistants (35 males and 45 females) at a large midwestern university served as subjects. They performed various counseling functions under the close supervision of one counseling psychologist and several doctoral candidates in counseling psychology.

Perception scores differed according to the counselor's attributes. The 40 counselors judged by supervisors as the more effective counselors rated the disabled similarly to normals. In contrast, perceptions of normals and disabled by the 40 less effective counselors differed significantly according to their sex. The males rated the disabled less favorably and the females rated them more favorably than they rated normal persons. The authors conclude that attitudes toward the disabled are important service-delivery factors and should be consciously dealt with in counselor training and in on-the-job supervision.

47. Corner, Ronald C., and Piliavin, June A. "As Others See Us: Attitudes of Physically Handicapped and Normals Toward Own and Other Groups." *Rehabilitation Literature*, 36, 7 (July 1975): 206-221, 225.

The three groups of subjects in this study were 34 physically normal males, 34 physically disabled patients of less than one year's duration, and 15 patients who had been physically disabled two to three years. The findings were as follows:
(1) Physically normal subjects rated physically handicapped persons more favorably than they do physically normal persons.
(2) Recently physically disabled patients hold similar attitudes as do physically normal persons.
(3) The long-term physically disabled patients hold the least favorable attitudes to the physically handicapped persons.

48. Croog, Sidney H., and Levine, Sol. "Religious Identity and Response to Serious Illness: A Report on Heart Patients." *Social Science and Medicine*, 6, 1 (February 1972): 17-32.

Using interview data gathered in three stages from 324 men in the Boston and Worcester, Massachusetts, areas, this study reports on aspects of the role of religion in providing support to individuals recovering from a life-threatening situation, a heart attack.

Over the first year following an attack, no significant changes were reported in level of religiosity, patterns of attendance at religious services, or in secular orientations to life and illness experiences. Among the three religious groups, Protestant, Catholic, and Jewish, definitions of disease etiology were highly secular. The heart attack did not alter religious or secular attitudes nor did it lead to increased dependency on religious institutions or clergy.

49. Croog, Sydney H.; Lipson, Alberta; and Levine, Sol. "Help Patterns in Severe Illness: The Roles of Kin Network, Non-Family Resources and Institutions." *Journal of Marriage and the Family*, 34, 1 (February 1972): 32-41.

This study related the patterns of support reported by men in an urban area who experienced their first myocardial infarction. 293 men who were patients in 26 hospitals in the Greater Boston and Worcester, Massachusetts, areas were the subjects of this study. They were interviewed about use of resources while severely ill. Findings revealed heavy use of resources while severely ill. Aside from use of medical and hospital service for immediate care and supervision, patients reported minimal contact with agencies and professionals. There was a lack of association between help pattern and perceived illness setbacks, social chaos, and ethnic origins. Findings are used to reject the notion of the apparent structural isolation of the nuclear family in time of crisis.

50. Croog, S.H.; Shapiro, D.S.; and Levine, S. "Denial Among Heart Patients: An Empirical Study." *Psychosomatic Medicine*, 33 (September 10, 1971): 385-397.

Of the 345 men under treatment for about three weeks after their first myocardial infarction, 20 percent were classified as denying their heart condition. Deniers and nondeniers were compared. Findings indicated that deniers were more likely to be Jewish and Italian than British and Irish. Deniers were also most likely to disavow possessing unfavorable personality traits when compared to nondeniers. The differences between the two groups continued to be present one year after the heart attack, suggesting a persistent phenomenon.

The Studies

51. D'Affletti, Judith Gregorie, and Swanson, Donna. "Group Sessions for the Wives of Home-Hemodialysis Patients." *American Journal of Nursing*, 75, 4 (April 1975): 633-635.

    The study reports on group sessions for wives of men on dialysis. Discussed are impact of dialysis on marital communication, uncertainty as to children's role in dialysis, wives' feelings of depression and isolation, and wives' problems in attempts to deal with guilt. Emotional support groups for family members are presented as an important part of overall dialysis treatment.

52. Dalton, Raymond F., Jr., and Latz, Adolph. "Vocational Placement: The Pennsylvania Rehabilitation Center." *Rehabilitation Literature*, 39, 11-12 (November 12, 1978): 336-339.

    A study of patients discharged from the vocational training center of Johnston Rehabilitation Center was undertaken. Patients completed the training during fiscal years 1973, 1974, and 1975. Findings indicated the following:
    (1) There was no relationship between placement success and sex, age, marital status, or race.
    (2) Placement in employment was related to program completion.
    (3) Program completion led to a higher degree of placement in employment in the areas in which patients were trained.

53. Daniel, Hal J., III, and Alston, Paul P. "Vocational Rehabilitation Counselor's Rankings of the Relative Severity of Profound Hearing Loss." *Journal of Rehabilitation of the Deaf*, 4, 4 (April 1971): 47-52.

    This article assesses the impact of handicap by having experienced rehabilitation personnel rank various disability conditions according to the severity of handicap presented in vocational, educational, and social areas. Nine disorders were ranked by 150 vocational rehabilitation counselors and supervisors. Emphasis is on ranking of hearing loss as a disability. The raters felt that a profoundly deaf individual faces a relatively severe handicap in the education and social areas of functioning, but a less severe handicap in the vocational area. The authors suggest that vocational placement often does not demand hearing for satisfactory performance, whereas educational and social areas require a wider variety of behavior and skills, many of which can be performed more easily with the benefit of hearing. Planning for the deaf should take these differential difficulties into consideration.

54. Daniels, Lloyd K. "Covert Reinforcement and Hypnosis in Modification of Attitudes Toward Physically Disabled Persons and Generalizations to the Emotionally Disturbed." *Psychological Reports*, 38 (1976): 554.

51 subjects were assigned to each of three experimental groups (covert reinforcement, hypnosis, and waiting control) which met for one-hour sessions for six weeks. All subjects completed the Attitude Toward Disabled Persons Scale and the Opinions About Mental Illness Scale. Results indicated that positive direct change in attitude occurred in all three groups toward physically disabled and emotionally disturbed persons. No significant differences were found among the three groups.

55. Dar, H.; Winter, S.T.; and Tal, Y. "Families of Children with Cleft Lips and Palates: Concerns and Counselling." *Developmental Medicine and Child Neurology*, 16, 4 (August 1974): 513-517.

This is a report on a survey of 51 families of children with cleft lip and/or palate. The paper focuses on the principal concerns of parents. The researchers note how concerns change as the child develops and matures. Counseling as it relates to these concerns is discussed.

56. Davis, Julia. "Performance of Young Hearing-Impaired Children on a Test of Basic Concepts." *Journal of Speech and Hearing Research*, 17, 3 (September 1974): 342-351.

The Boehm Test of Basic Concepts was administered to 24 hard-of-hearing children and 24 normal hearing children, all of whom were between the ages of 6 and 9. The hard-of-hearing attended public schools. The results indicated that children with greater hearing losses scored significantly lower on the Boehm test than children with mild hearing losses or normal hearing. The author uses these findings to support the premise that hearing-impaired children are delayed in academic development.

57. De-Nour, A. Kaplan. "Personality Factors Influencing Vocational Rehabilitation." *Archives of General Psychiatry*, 32 (May 1975): 573-577.

This is a report of psychiatric evaluation and follow-ups of 50 male patients with chronic renal conditions. The purpose of the study was to uncover personality factors that influence vocational rehabilitation. Findings included: there is a high tendency to decrease in functioning following commencement of dialysis; it is possible to predict rehabilitation and functional decreases even in patients who are functioning well; work satisfaction, predialysis functioning, sick role, and dependency needs all predict vocational rehabilitation. The findings indicate that best vocational rehabilitation is related to earliness of onset of treatment.

58. De-Nour, Atara Kaplan. "Adolescents' Adjustment to Chronic Hemodialysis." *American Journal of Psychiatry*, 136, 4A (April 1979): 430-433.

Using pre- and post-dialysis interviews, this research compares the adjustment of 18 adolescents on chronic hemodialysis to that of 63 adult patients on hemodialysis. Adolescents followed medical regimen less well, had a significantly lower vocational rehabilitation, and had more restricted social activities. Adolescents were more hostile and aggressive, but exhibited fewer psychiatric complications. Changes in body function and physical appearance were more problematic for the adolescents. The study demonstrates that chronic disease is especially difficult for adolescents because it creates stress in areas particularly problematic for that age group.

59. DeNour, A.K., and Czackes, J.W. "Personality Factors in Chronic Hemodialysis Patients Causing Noncompliance with Medical Regimen." *Psychosomatic Medicine*, 34 (July 8, 1972): 333-344.

43 patients on chronic hemodialysis, who did not comply with the medical diet regimen, were studied. Findings indicated that noncompliance was associated with the gains (primary and secondary) from adoption of the sick role. Low frustration level was also associated with noncompliance.

60. Dibner, Andrew S. "Semi-integrated Camping for the Physically Handicapped Child." *Rehabilitation Psychology*, 20, 2 (Summer 1973): 84-93.

This study reports on the effects of a camping experience for handicapped boys when semi-integrated into a setting for physically normal boys. Effects on both the handicapped boys and the camp counselors are reported. The physically handicapped boys showed positive gains in self-concept that exceeded those of the non-handicapped boys. Most of the handicapped boys had successful relationships with the nonhandicapped boys and 90% had good or better relationships with their handicapped peers. The more severe the handicap the less was the change of a good relationship with the non-handicapped boys. The situation with the counselors was somewhat different. Those who dealt mainly with normal boys in the camp improved their attitudes toward disability, while the counselors in the handicapped unit were less positive after the experience. The author suggests ways for counselors to deal with their feelings on disability.

61. Dikeman, S., and Matthews, C.G. "Effects of Major Motor Seizure Frequency upon Cognitive-Intellectual Functions in Adults." *Epilepsia*, 18 (1977): 21-29.

Wechsler Adult Intelligence Scale was administered to 72 adult patients with epilepsy. They were divided into three groups according to frequency of seizures. The groups were matched for seizure duration and age of onset variables. On 7 of the 14 variables employed, significant differences among groups were found. The highest-frequency seizure group scored the lowest. The results support the conclusion that increased frequency of major motor seizures is associated with impaired cognitive functioning.

62. Dikeman, S.; Matthews, C.G.; and Harley, J.P. "The Effects of Early Versus Late Onset of Major Motor Epilepsy upon Cognitive-Intellectual Performance." *Epilepsia*, 16 (1975): 73-81.

Performance on the Wechsler Adult Intelligence Scale was investigated in two groups of adult subjects with major motor epilepsy of early (0 to 5 years) and later (17 to 50 years) onset. The early onset group scored significantly lower on 9 of the 14 measures that comprise the Wechsler Scale than did the later onset group. The results support the conclusion that early age of onset of major motor seizures is more apt to result in impairment of mental abilities in adult life than is later onset of seizures.

63. Dixon, Jane K. "Coping with Prejudice: Attitudes of Handicapped Persons Toward the Handicapped." *Journal of Chronic Diseases*, 30, 5 (May 1977): 307-322.

In an exploration of the amount of prejudice handicapped people feel toward other handicapped people, compared to that felt by nonhandicapped people, it was found that a distinction should be made between relatively visible handicaps and relatively invisible handicaps. People with amputation, spinal injury, and stroke (highly visible) had positive attitudes, but arthritics and emotionally disturbed persons did not. The results suggest that promoting opportunities for association with persons with like handicaps would be beneficial to those with highly visible handicaps; but for the less visibly handicapped such a strategy would not be useful. Study data is provided and extensively referenced.

64. Donaldson, Joy, and Martinson, Melton C. "Modifying Attitudes Toward Physically Disabled Persons." *Exceptional Children*, 43, 6 (March 1977): 337-341.

120 nondisabled students from introductory psychology classes were randomly assigned to four experimental groups, with 15 males and 15 females assigned to each group. The results suggested that live and video presentation, as contrasted with video only, had a positive impact on changing attitudes as measured by the Attitude Toward Disabled Persons Scale.

65. Dorner, S. "The Relationship of Physical Handicap to Stress in Families with an Adolescent with Spina Bifida." *Developmental Medicine and Child Neurology*, 17, 6 (December 1975): 765-776.

This report is based on interview data gathered from the parents of 63 adolescents with spina bifida. In the adolescents impaired mobility seems to be associated with feelings of depression and social isolation. Males with urinary appliances feel this isolation and depression more than other adolescents. Parents feel socially restricted due to mobility concerns for the child. No association was found between the child's physical problems and depression in the mother.

66. Dyer, Elaine; Cole, Roberta C.; Franklin, Susan; Ishida, Dianne N.; Nugent, Lynn H.; Chalfant, Anna Lee; Donahue, Elizabeth M.; Hickok, Nell; Kunishi, Marilyn M.; and Plaisted, Sally. "Factors Related to Diabetic Clients' Knowledge." *Psychological Reports*, 44 (1979): 683-690.

114 diabetic clients were studied to determine relationships between clients' knowledge and demographic factors. High pre-test scores were obtained by clients who (a) were better educated, (b) had diabetes longer, and (c) were younger. High post-test scores were obtained by clients who (a) were better educated, (b) were younger, (c) had read more written materials about diabetes, and (d) had received instruction in an outpatient course. Authors argue that the findings support concept that maximum learning occurs when clients attend diabetic courses after discharge from the hospital.

67. Eaglestein, A. Solomon. "The Social Acceptance of Blind High School Students in an Integrated School." *New Outlook for the Blind*, 69, 12 (December 1975): 447-451.

This study reports on nine blind students studying in an integrated high school in Israel. The purpose is to determine academic standing and social acceptance. School grades were average and the blind students were generally well integrated into the social life of their classes. The study also found that as length of exposure to blind students increased, their social acceptance decreased.

68. Ebert, Priscilla R.; McWilliams, Betty Jane; and Woolf, Gerald. "A Comparison of the Written Language Ability of Cleft Palate and Normal Children." *Cleft Palate Journal*, 11 (January 1974): 17-20.

23 children with palatal clefts were matched with 23 children who had no history of oral pathology or speech disorders. The patient and comparison group were similar in their written language skills as measured by Myklebust Picture Story Language Test. The findings lead the authors to conclude that significantly lower scores on verbal IQ measures for the patient group indicated expressive, not cognitive, deficiency.

69. Ehrlich, Carol; Shapiro, Esther; Kimball, Bud D.; and Huttner, Muriel. "Communication Skills in Five-Year-Old Children with High-Risk Neonatal Histories." *Journal of Speech and Hearing*, 16, 3 (September 1973): 522-529.

Speech, language, auditory, and intellectual development were assessed in 81 five-year-old children with one or more of the following high-risk histories: birth weight less than 2500 grams, gestational age less than 38 weeks, RH or BO blood incompatibility, and respiratory distress. Tests included the Peabody Picture Vocabulary Test, Templin-Darley Articulation Screening Test, Wechsler Intelligence Scale for Children and audiological examination. Respiratory distress or abnormal birth weight and gestational age led to the greatest incidence of disability. Despite normal intelligence, 54% of the children needed special help. Findings suggest the need for early identification and intervention to avoid accumulated deficits.

70. Elder, Ruth, and Acheson, Roy M. "New Haven Survey of Joint Diseases XIV. Social Class and Behavior in Response to Symptoms of Osteoarthrosis." *Milbank Memorial Fund Quarterly*, 48, 4 (October 1970): 449-502.

What social patterns of behavior are associated with symptoms of osteoarthrosis (arthritis or rheumatism)? With whom do sufferers talk about the complaint? What, if anything, do they do about it? To which trained people do they turn for help? Are they satisfied with the help they get? Do people in different social classes respond differently to this health situation?

Interviews with 2,199 people, from a pool of 45 to 64 year olds who have morning stiffness, resulted in 229 subjects. Most admitted they discusss their symptoms with other laypersons, particularly with individuals they feel had similar complaints. These are casual, unplanned conversations, but through them individuals learn how to cope. Reports from persons of the upper class indicate that they are less likely to dwell on symptoms in conversation, but more willing to do so if the other person has similar complaints. Upper-class persons are more likely to go directly to a specialist than to a general practitioner. This supports research that indicates that lower-class people are more likely to turn to druggists, nurses, etc., for health care advice.

Respondents most often use heat and aspirin; there is little variation by class. Upper-class persons report using these with the blessing of their physician. Both groups use home remedies.

71. Evans, Joseph. "Attitudes toward the Disabled and Aggression." *Perceptual and Motor Skills*, 37 (December 1973): 834.

20 juvenile delinquents were compared with 20 juvenile non-delinquents on their attitude toward disabled persons. The delinquents were significantly less accepting of disabled persons than were the juvenile non-delinquents. The author concluded that aggression as a personality variable is negatively related to positive attitudes toward the disabled.

72. Feinman, Saul. "Do Sighted People Respond to Different Levels of Visual Loss?" *Journal of Visual Impairment and Blindness*, 73, 5 (May 1979): 185-190.

The study seeks to discover whether sighted people discriminate between levels of vision loss. The experimental variables were degree of vision impairment and age of impaired individual. Respondents held higher expectations for sighted than partially sighted persons, and higher for partially sighted than totally sightless persons. Older persons were given lower expectations. Respondents did not differentiate the term "blind" from the partially sighted or totally sightless.

73. Ferro, Jerard M., and Allen, Harry A. "Sexuality: the Effects of Physical Impairment." *Rehabilitation Counseling Bulletin*, 20, 2 (December 1976): 148-151.

The purpose of the study was to assess the attitudes and feelings of physically disabled college students concerning their own sexuality and some aspects of sexual behavior. The patient group consisted of 23 college students at Southern Illinois University who were in wheelchairs. The comparison group consisted of 27 students selected at random and matched with the patient group. Semantic differential format was used as the stimulus. There were no differences between the two groups in relation to attitudes and feelings about sexual behavior. The disabled group did score significantly lower in relation to feelings of sexuality as compared to the nondisabled group.

74. Fleck, Robert E.; Richardson, Stephen A.; and Ronald, Linda. "Physical Appearance Cues and Interpersonal Attraction in Children." *Child Development*, 45, 2 (June 1974): 305-310.

The findings of two studies of 9- to 14-year-old boys at a summer camp for two weeks supported the proposition that differences in perceived physical attractiveness were systematically related to social acceptance. Furthermore, there was a positive association between sociometric status (friendship selection) and physical attractiveness.

75. Flynn, Robert J., and Salamone, Paul R. "Performance of the MMPI in Predicting Rehabilitation Outcome: A Discriminant Analysis, Double Cross-Validation Assessment." *Rehabilitation Literature*, 38, 1 (January 1977): 12-15.

Minnesota Multiphasic Personality Inventory data was obtained on 128 successfully and 128 unsuccessfully rehabilitated clients of the Minneapolis Rehabilitation Center. The results do not suggest the use of the MMPI on a regular basis for prediction of outcome.

76. Fogel, Max L., and Rosillo, Ronald H. "Relationship Between Intellectual Factors and Coping in Physical Rehabilitation." *Rehabilitation Counseling Bulletin*, 17, 2 (December 1973): 68-78.

122 patients with different types of physical disabilities were studied to test the relationship between intellectual factors and improvement in physical rehabilitation. Intellectual functioning as measured by WISC, length of stay in hospital, sex, and age were not associated with improvement in rehabilitation. The improvement in rehabilitation was assessed on an objective rating scale for degree of change in patient from admission to discharge.

77. Fox, Donna; Lynch, Joan; and Brookshire, Bonnie. "Selected Developmental Factors of Cleft Palate Children Between Two and 33 Months of Age." *Cleft Palate Journal*, 15, 3 (July 1978): 239-245.

The purpose of this investigation was to ascertain if developmental delay could be observed in 24 children with cleft palate below the age of three years when compared to a matched control group. The children were administered the Denver Developmental Screening Scale and Receptive Expressive Emergent Language (REEL) Scale. The patient group scored significantly lower on the two subscales of the REEL and one of the subscales of the Denver Developmental. The authors argue for early intervention to prevent developmental delays from becoming greater with the passage of time.

78. Franklin, Billy J. "Birth Order and Tendency to 'Adopt the Sick Role.'" *Psychological Reports*, 33 (1973): 437-438.

   152 college student volunteers were administered a series of biographical questions determining birth order and a three-item measure of tendency to "adopt the sick role." In the three hypothetical situations, first borns had a significantly greater tendency to adopt the role of being sick than did later borns confronted with similar symptoms. The author argues that these findings support the premise that parents of first borns are more sensitive to symptoms of illness and are more likely to seek the aid of a medical authority than parents of later borns. Therefore, first borns are more likely to "adopt the sick role."

79. Freeman, Roger D.; Malkin, Susan F.; and Hastings, Jane O. "Psychosocial Problems of Deaf Children and Their Families: A Comparative Study." *American Annals of the Deaf*, 120, 4 (August 1975): 391-405.

   The study sample consisted of 120 prelingually deaf children (ages 5 to 15 years) and their families, representing almost all the cases in the Greater Vancouver region, and a matched hearing group. Information was obtained by means of parent and school questionnaires, psychological testing, home visit observations, and a semistructured parent interview, in addition to a review of available medical data.

   In comparison with the hearing group, deaf children were found to be socially disadvantaged due to indirect as well as direct consequences of deafness. Significant differences were found in early hospitalization, frequency of home moves, certain areas of behavior, activities permitted by parents, amount of play, and parental expectations. Contrary to previous clinical lore, divorce and separation were not common. Delay in medical diagnosis, the effects of associated brain damage, and the influence of educational controversies are other factors that make it difficult to sort out the inevitable primary consequences of childhood deafness from the secondary social, medical, and educational factors.

80. Freeston, B.M. "An Enquiry into the Effect of a Spina Bifida Child upon Family Life." *Developmental Medicine and Child Neurology*, 13, 4 (August 1971): 456-461.

Families of two groups of children were interviewed to assess the impact of a child with spinal bifida upon the family and also to see how existing social services meet family needs. The discussion focuses on impact of child's birth, genetic counseling, marital relationship, and financial stress.

81. Galbreath, Judith, and Feinberg, Lawrence B. "Ambiguity and Attitudes Toward Employment of the Disabled: A Multi-dimensional Study." *Rehabilitation Psychology*, 20, 4 (Winter 1973): 165-174.

This study seeks to answer whether persons who are intolerant of ambiguity react in a generalized way to all disabled persons, or whether their responses are a function of the ambiguity characteristics of the disability and the context in which the disability is perceived. A tolerance-intolerance of ambiguity scale was administered to college students. They were divided into groups based on their score. They were also exposed to vignettes describing a disabled job applicant and a potential employment situation. The vignettes varied in terms of ambiguity. The students were then scored on an Attitude Toward Disabled Persons scale. Subjects high on intolerance of ambiguity scored higher in terms of negative attitudes. Disability type did not influence the response of the intolerant types. Tolerant subjects were more affected by disability type. The findings have implications both for the disabled and for others in positions of rehabilitation counseling and vocational placement.

82. Gall, John C., Jr.; Hayward, James R.; Harper, Mary L.; and Garn, S.M. "Studies of Dysmorphogenesis in Children with Oral Clefts: I. Relationship Between Clinical Findings and School Performance." *Cleft Palate Journal*, 9, 4 (October 1972): 326-334.

101 school-age children with cleft lip and/or palate who were patients at the University of Michigan Cleft Palate Center were studied during 1969-71. Children with additional dysmorphogenetic features (e.g., congenital ear disease, malformed hands) were more likely to have impaired school performance than children with only a cleft lip and/or palate. This finding supports the premise that the number, not kind, of handicaps is important in influencing a patient's behavioral adjustment.

83. Gallagher, Patricia A., and Heim, Ruth E. "The Classroom Application of Behavioral Modification Principles for Multiply Handicapped Blind Students." *New Outlook for the Blind*, 68, 10 (December 1974): 447-453.

This article reports three studies of multiply handicapped blind students enrolled in a special class in a residential school for blind children. Behavior modification was used to decrease negative and increase positive comments, to increase independent school seat work, and to learn mobility skills.

84. Garrity, Thomas F. "Vocational Adjustment After First Myocardial Infarction: Comparative Assessment of Several Variables Suggested in the Literature." *Social Science and Medicine*, 7, 9 (September 1973): 705-717.

The researcher studied literature on vocational adjustment after cardiac and other illnesses to determine factors associated with returning to work. He then tested the identified variables on 58 white males from the Durham, North Carolina, area. All had survived their first myocardial infarction for at least six months.

Return to work was predicted by patient's perception of health status, social class, and feeling of control over fate. Amount of weekly work involvement after attack was related to amount of weekly work involvement before attack and feeling of pressures from significant others. The results are presented in terms of strategies to improve post-attack vocational adjustment.

85. Gilder, Rodman; Buschman, Penelope R.; Sitarz, Annaliese L.; and Wolff, James A. "Group Therapy with Parents of Children with Leukemia." *American Journal of Psychotherapy*, 32, 2 (April 1978): 276-287.

This is an observational report on a six-year experience of group therapy for parents of children with leukemia. The purpose of the group is to strengthen the role of parents, doctors, and nurses. The therapy is viewed as a preventive measure to resolve family stress and as a way to strengthen staff in their management of families. In this group the active participation of a hematologist to clarify information and work through emotional attitudes was viewed as a plus.

86. Gillman, Arthur E., and Goddard, Dorothy Rose. "The 20-Year Outcome of Blind Children Two Years Old and Younger: A Preliminary Survey." *New Outlook for the Blind*, 68, 1 (January 1974): 1-7.

This article reports on a longitudinal-outcome study of 77 blind children registered with one agency for the blind in 1949-1950. Twenty-five percent were still active with the agency, 20 percent were institutionalized, 15 percent had attended college. Subjects became more aware of functional vision as they grew older. Actual changes in visual acuity were minimal. As they grew older some of the children developed additional handicaps.

87. Gillman, Arthur E.; Simon, Ellen Perlman; and Shinn, Eugene B. "An Outcome Study of an Intensive Rehabilitation Training Program for Young Adults." *Journal of Visual Impairment and Blindness*, 72, 10 (December 1978): 388-392.

This study is an ex post facto evaluation of 44 multiple handicapped adults who participated in an intensive training program at the New York Association for the Blind (Lighthouse). These adults could not use other rehabilitation programs. Data collected at entry, exit, and follow-up indicates that most clients expressed satisfaction with the program and most retained independent living, mobility, and employment skills long after program exit. Among factors most influencing success in the program were: entry into program at an early age, preferably under 25; better or more as opposed to less or no vision. Persons unoccupied for long time periods before program entry did poorest.

88. Gilmore, Stuart I. "Social and Vocational Acceptability of Esophageal Speakers Compared to Normal Speakers." *Journal of Speech and Hearing Research*, 17, 4 (December 1974): 599-607.

A group of 480 business and professional men evaluated four speakers on one social (familial and community) and three vocational criteria. Laryngectomees with esophageal speech were rated as less acceptable socially and as able to handle significantly fewer jobs than were normal speakers. Introductory information about esophageal speech resulted in higher ratings of social acceptability, number of jobs relegated to speakers and the prestige associated with those jobs. However, increased information decreased the subject's willingness to place the worker who had had a laryngectomy in a position involving public contact.

89. Glass, Lillian, and Starr, Clark D. "A Study of Relationships Between Judgments of Speech and Appearance of Patients with Orofacial Clefts." *Cleft Palate Journal*, 16 (1979): 436-440.

   A series of six studies was designed to examine the interaction between a subject's appearance and nasal speech upon judgments of independent raters. Results of two-way analysis of variance failed to support the idea that appearance has an effect on ratings of nasal speech. Results of a two-way analysis of variance indicated that nasality had an effect on ratings of appearance. As the severity of nasality increased, ratings of attractiveness decreased. Results imply that a decrease in nasality may enhance the way persons with a cleft lip are perceived cosmetically.

90. Gogstad, A.C., and Kjellman, Anna Malmer. "Rehabilitation Prognosis Related to Clinical and Social Factors in Brain Injured of Different Etiology." *Social Science and Medicine*, 10, 6 (June 1976): 283-288.

   This study reports on 72 patients with brain lesions of sudden onset but different etiology. Most were good candidates for return to work, but after 18-24 months only 40% were working. Most patients previously worked in unqualified jobs and had social and psychological problems. The research reports no clear evidence of significant correlations between various clinical, social, and psychological variables and the results of rehabilitation. High age, from 40 to 45 years and up, was considered a disadvantage, but this may reflect social factors of age rather than biological changes. Rapid rehabilitation efforts are reported as more desirable than delayed efforts. The uncertainty of rehabilitation from brain disorders is underscored.

91. Goldberg, Richard T. "Vocational and Social Adjustment After Laryngectomy." *Scandinavian Journal of Rehabilitation Medicine*, 7, 1 (1975): 1-8.

   This study examined the vocational and social adjustment of 62 persons with cancer of the larynx. Predisability data were obtained by interview on 14 measures that assessed the vocational, social, and home adjustment prior to cancer. Postdisability data were obtained after laryngectomy by interview on 21 measures of adjustment. Additional measures included severity of laryngeal cancer classified by clinical stages, total or partial laryngectomy, presence of radiation therapy, presence of speech, months since surgery, age, sex, education, and marital status. The best predictors of vocational and social adjustment after laryngectomy were: remotivation, realism, rehabilitation outlook, previous vocational plans, highest educational grade, educational plans, and acquisition of speech. There were no significant differences in adjustment among patients in different clinical stages.

92. Goldberg, Richard T.; Bernstein, Norman R.; and Crosby, Roberta. "Vocational Development of Adolescents with Burn Injury." *Rehabilitation Counseling Bulletin*, 18, 3 (March 1975): 140-146.

34 adolescents with burn injury were the sample for this study. Subjects were interviewed on the Goldberg Scale of Vocational Development. Severity of facial disfigurement negatively correlated with rehabilitation outlook and career planning. The findings of this study again illustrate the importance of facial appearance for entry into many occupations.

93. Goldberg, R.T.; Isralsky, M.; and Shwachma, H. "Vocational Development and Adjustment of Adolescents with Cystic Fibrosis." *Archives of Physical Medicine and Rehabilitation*, 60 (August 1979): 369-374.

25 adolescents with cystic fibrosis were compared with normal adolescents of the same age (12 to 16 years) and educational grade (7th to 9th) on several measures of vocational development and adjustment. The patient group scored significantly lower than the normal adolescents in relation to vocational and educational aspirations. The patient group, however, scored significantly higher in relation to commitment to work, work values, and awareness of occupational information. The authors argue that these findings are due to the fact that work was the only outlet for the patients with cystic fibrosis.

94. Goldberg, Richard T.; Satow, Kay L.; and Bigwood, A. Winton. "Vocational Adjustment, Work Interests, Work Values, and Rehabilitation Outlook of Women on Long Term Hemodialysis." *Rehabilitation Psychology*, 20, 1 (Summer 1973): 94-101.

Interviews with 22 women on long-term hemodialysis were utilized to ascertain their vocational plans, work interests, and values prior to and following dialysis. All women interviewed were either employed workers or homemakers. Single employed women continued their work schedules with little or no disruption. Working wives more often had to give up their careers due to nonavailability of extra time for working outside the home. Those women who were full-time homemakers prior to dialysis remained the same. Men generally are encouraged to maintain their careers by the work ethic, whereas women, particularly if they have competing responsibilities, seem to substitute for career.

95. Golin, Anne K. "Stimulus Variables in the Measurement of Attitudes Toward Disability." *Rehabilitation Counseling Bulletin*, 14, 1 (September 1970): 20-26.

With semantic differential rating scales to measure response, 114 university students enrolled in an undergraduate psychology course were queried on their attitudes toward the disabled. The author hypothesizes that, if negative stereotyping is reduced by presentation of favorable information about a disabled person, then the presentation of negative information should serve to reinforce negative stereotyping and elicit unfavorable attitudes. Half of the students were given a little information on a disabled person and half received a larger amount. In these groups, half were presented favorable information and half unfavorable information. It was found that the favorableness of information given the subject did have a significant effect upon measured attitudes. However, the hypothesis of increased negative attitudes toward disability due to reinforcement of negative stereotyping by presentation of unfavorable information was not supported.

96. Gottheil, Edward; McGurn, Wealtha C.; and Pollak, Otto. "Awareness and Disengagement in Cancer Patients." *American Journal of Psychiatry*, 136, 5 (May 1979): 632-636.

This study compares cancer patients to other chronic-disease patients in terms of awareness of condition and disengagement. Both cancer and noncancer patients who were aware were more engaged. Aware patients lived longer if they were engaged; patients who were unaware lived longer if they were disengaged. Unresolved questions remain as to the effect of awareness. It may benefit some patients but not others.

97. Grace, Harry A. "A System Approach to Employment After Orthopedic Rehabilitation." *Rehabilitation Counseling Bulletin*, 13, 3 (March 1970): 261-270.

This study was designed to determine how employers viewed orthopedically handicapped persons as prospective workers. 144 mailed questionnaires were analyzed. Employment was associated with size of firm (larger one), type of work (manufacturing firms were more likely to hire people with social limitations), and experience with disabled workers (more experienced employers are less concerned with physical limitations).

98. Green, Sara C.; Kappes, Bruno M.; and Parrioh, Thomas S. "Attitudes of Educators Toward Handicapped and Non-Handicapped Children." *Psychological Reports*, 44 (1979): 829-830.

111 educators (56 from institutional settings and 55 from public schools) were administered four versions of the Personal Attitude Inventory for "gifted children," "normal children," "mentally retarded children," and "severely multiple handicapped children." No significant differences existed between the two handicapped conditions, but both were significantly different from either "gifted" or "normal children." The authors conclude that the findings support the notion that educators, regardless of institutional settings or professional status, appear to have negative feelings toward handicapped children.

99. Greer, Bobby G. "Attitudes Toward Different Types of Deviant Persons." *Rehabilitation Literature*, 36, 6 (June 1975): 182-184.

99 special education teachers attending a summer inservice training workshop were administered the Disability Opinion Scale and Social Distance Survey. The findings show that the subjects perceive physically and mentally disabled patients as more favorable than patients who are alcoholics. The teachers were also more reluctant to give special consideration to the first two groups than to the alcoholics. Together, findings support the premise that the subjects perceived the physically and mentally disabled as having a more favorable prognosis.

100. Haber, Lawrence D. "Some Parameters for Social Policy in Disability: A Cross National Comparison." *Milbank*

Memorial Fund Quarterly, 51, 3 (Summer 1973): 319-336.

This article stresses that if an effective public policy relative to disability is to be enacted, then there must be agreement between conceptual and operational measures of the term "disability." The author demonstrates how the prevalence and level of severity of disability vary in national studies depending on the measures used. Disability statistics from five nations are compared, with particular attention to differences in measurement and their effect on levels of comparative studies using common methods and criteria.

101. Hall, Penelope K., and Tomblin, J. Bruce. "A Follow-Up Study of Children with Articulation and Language Disorders." *Journal of Speech and Hearing Disorders*, 43, 2 (May 1978): 227-241.

18 language-impaired and 18 articulation-impaired children were followed up with respect to communication skills and educational performance 13 to 20 years after their initial contact with a speech and hearing clinic. According to the parents, 9 language-impaired subjects continued to exhibit communication problems as adults, compared to only one articulation-impaired subject. Educational testing at the secondary level indicated that the language-impaired group consistently achieved at a lower level than the articulation-impaired group, particularly in reading. Language-impaired subjects have deficiencies in the ability to use language in either spoken or written form. Therefore, these deficiencies help explain the decreased scores of the language-impaired in learning. Findings support the concern about the impact of language deficits on educational achievement.

102. Halverson, Charles F., Jr., and Victor, James B. "Minor Physical Anomalies and Problem Behavior in Elementary School Children." *Child Development*, 47, 1 (May 1976): 281-285.

The subjects were 100 elementary school students, 50 male and 50 female, in a predominantly white, middle-class suburban school. All subjects were randomly selected and independently assessed for minor physical anomalies, such as widely spaced eyes and wide gaps between first and second toes. Problem behavior was measured by the Quay and Paterson Checklist and teacher's ratings. Scores on these two measures were related to the incidence of minor physical anomalies for boys. Friendship selection was related to the incidence of minor physical anomalies for both sexes.

103. Hansen, Philip, and Keogh, Barbara K. "Medical Characteristics of Children with Educational Handicaps." *Clinical Pediatrics*, (December 1971): 726-730.

252 educationally handicapped children were evaluated by pediatricians. Findings indicated a higher frequency of physical-medical problems with educationally handicapped children, especially those from lower socioeconomic backgrounds. The authors conclude that these findings provide support for the premise that there are biological contributions to learning problems.

104. Harasymew, Stefan J.; Horne, Marcia D.; and Lewis, Sally C. "A Longitudinal Study of Disability Group Acceptance." *Rehabilitation Literature*, 37, 4 (April 76): 98-102.

The attitudes of the general population toward 22 disability groups were studied. 4,459 subjects comprised the various samples and the research spanned eight years. The major finding was the stability of preference in attitudes regardless of demographic indicators of the sample and the type of attitude-measuring instrument used. The hierarchy of attitude preference was physical, sensory, psychogenic (e.g., mental problems), and social (e.g., drug problems).

105. Hartlage, L.C., and Green, J.B. "The Relation of Parental Attitudes to Academic and Social Achievement in Epileptic Children." *Epilepsia*, 13 (1972): 21-26.

Parental attitudes were correlated with several variables related to academic and social achievement in 54 epileptic children. Parental attitudes were assessed by the Parent Attitude Research Instrument. Positive social development as measured by the Vineland Social Maturity Scale was associated with parental attitudes involving strictness and emphasis on adherence to parental wishes, coupled with a regard for the child as a person. Frequency of seizures was negatively correlated with social development but was not correlated with academic achievement. The type of seizure was not significantly correlated with either academic achievement or social development. The authors argue that parental attitudes may be more important than the condition per se in determining a patient's prognosis.

106. Havill, Stephen James. "Sociometric Status of Visually Handicapped Students in Public School Classes." *American Foundation for the Blind Research Bulletin*, 20 (March 1970): 57-81.

This study sought to determine the sociometric status of visually handicapped children integrated into regular classes. The predictive value of grade level, sex, degree of impairment, school achievement, socioeconomic level, amount of time spent in the integrated situation, and type of special service received in determining sociometric status was investigated. The major finding of the study was that the visually handicapped were of lower sociometric status and less accepted than classmates with normal vision. Above-average achievement and itinerant service were factors which had a positive effect on status. The other variables were not especially helpful in predicting sociometric status.

107. Heijbel, J., and Bohman M. "Benign Epilepsy of Chidren with Centrotemporal EEG Foci: Intelligence, Behavior, and Social Adjustment." *Epilepsia*, 16 (1975): 679-687.

16 children between the ages of seven and twelve with benign epilepsy and centrotemporal EEG foci were matched with classmates for age and sex. There were no differences between the two groups on the three measures employed. The epileptic seizures did not have any effect on the children's intelligence. These findings suggest that this type of epilepsy with medical treatment has probably reduced the risk of behavioral disorders in these children.

108. Hellmuth, George A. "Cardiac Employees and their Immediate Supervisors." *Journal of Occupational Medicine*, 13, 4 (April 1971): 166-174.

This study reports on interviews with cardiac employees and their supervisors in a light manufacturing firm. Generalized information is reported on employee's attitudes toward supervisor's treatment of them in regard to the cardiac condition, the supervisor's own attitude toward the cardiac, and both worker's and supervisor's belief in the work ethic. The researcher examines factors in the plant environment that seem to lead to favorable interactions and attitudes between cardiac employees and employers/supervisors.

109. Henderson, David J.; Orth, Donald; Robson, Richard; and Stein, Joseph M. "Improved Work Classification in Post-Myocardial Infarction Rehabilitation." *Journal of Rehabilitation*, 43 (November/December 1977): 48-51.

To increase likelihood of returning to work after a heart attack, a pilot study of the effectiveness of achieving physiological competence was undertaken. 28 unemployed men who had experienced myocardial infarction were the subjects for the study. They were all volunteers and screened for willingness to cooperate. The findings indicated that 82% of the subjects completed the program. They had a higher physiological level of competence and a significantly higher return to work rate.

110. Hicks, John S., and Wieder, Daniel. "The Effects of Intergeneration Group Counseling on Clients and Parents in a Vocational Rehabilitation Agency." *Rehabilitation Literature*, 34, 12 (December 1973): 358-363, 368.

Two group counseling programs with cerebral palsy patients were evaluated. The experimental group met with parents and children together. In the control situation, parents and children met separately. Parents favored the experimental condition whereas the children favored the control situation.

111. Hill, Carole E. "Differential Perceptions of the Rehabilitation Process: A Comparison of Client and Personnel Incongruity in Two Categories of Chronic Illness." *Social Science and Medicine*, 12B, 1 (1978): 57-62.

Patient's perception concerning treatment and rehabilitation in two units of chronically ill, physically disabled clients, are presented against a background of the perceptions of the personnel in these units. Beliefs and behaviors of the two groups are shown to be incongruent. These incongruities are discussed in terms of medical and organizational models. The relevance of medical anthropology and a holistic approach to rehabilitation are argued.

112. Hoemann, Harry W. "Deaf Children's Use of Fingerspelling to Label Pictures of Common Objects: A Follow-Up Study." *Exceptional Children*, 40, 7 (April 1974): 519-520.

 52 children at a residential school for the deaf were tested two years after the introduction of fingerspelling. They were tested to assess the change, if any, on the children's acquisition of vocabulary. The results indicated that fingerspelling does have a positive impact on acquisition of vocabulary and that age is a key variable. The greatest gains were made by the youngest sample (ages 6 or 7), while the older sample (ages 8 or 9) showed no gains at all either in the use of fingerspelling or in spelling correctly.

113. Holcombe, Joan Lindall, and MacDonald, Robert Wesley. "Social Functioning of Artificial Kidney Patients." *Social Science and Medicine*, 7, 2 (February 1973): 109-119.

 This study investigated the social and family functioning of 23 Northwest Kidney Center patients and their spouses. Several variables were investigated, but emphasis was on depression, financial difficulty, and sexual satisfaction. Earlier studies identified these areas as problematic for dialysis patients. The objective was to see how one sample of patients describe their family and home life after dialysis is incorporated into their daily routine. On the average, patients had two years of home dialysis treatment.
 Patients generally felt more comfortable two years after home dialysis: they felt medically stable. Significantly more patients felt financially secure than did their spouses, while significantly more spouses reported vague insecurity. Areas of discomfort differed for patients and spouses. The patient group was more concerned about health, depression, and frustration. The spouses were concerned about feelings of depression, frustration, and vague insecurity. The nature of the feelings of depression differed for patient and spouse. For the patient there was greater emphasis on not reaching life goals; for the spouse the feelings centered on not feeling appreciated.
 Sexual fulfillment did not seem to be a problem for the sample group. However, when sexual enjoyment diminished, a highly significant association with extremely depressed feelings on the part of one or both parties resulted.

114. Howard, Jan, and Holman, Barbara L. "The Effects of Race and Occupation on Hypertensive Mortality." *Milbank Memorial Fund Quarterly*, 48, 3 (July 1970): 263-296.

The data reported here is secondary analysis of the Public Health Service 1963 report. Regardless of occupation and social class, nonwhites were found to have a higher mortality from hypertension than whites. The magnitude of the race difference in hypertension decreases with age. For both races, laborers have the highest mortality from hypertension. Nonwhites show more variability in mortality over the various occupations and classes than do whites.

115. Hyman, Herbert H.; Stokes, Janet; and Strauss, Helen M. "Occupational Aspirations Among the Totally Blind." *Social Forces*, 51, 4 (June 1973): 403-416.

This study is based on interviews with 102 blind children between the ages of 10 and 15 and their mothers or mother surrogates, as well as siblings of 50 of the children. In addition, supplemental samples of adults who were totally blinded before age eight were utilized. Comparison is offered on the racially variable aspirations of black versus white children. Blind children are reported to have high but not unrealistic aspirations. Black blind children have aspirations for self higher than those they recommend for an outstanding person, blind or sighted, and equal to those of white blind children. In assessing realistic achievement, the blind children frequently doubt they will achieve what they would like to. This is more often true for black blind children. The research also documents parents' desire to make aspirations of blind children a reality.

116. Hyman, Martin D. "Disability and Patients' Perceptions of Preferential Treatment: Some Preliminary Findings." *Journal of Chronic Diseases*, 24, 5 (August 1971): 329-342.

A study of 116 patients suspected of being in the early stages of chronic illness was undertaken to test the idea that chronic disease sets in motion social and psychosocial processes that impede medical efforts to maintain the patient at a maximum level of functioning. The study confirmed that preferential treatment and an associated protectiveness and socialization to the sick role may constitute one such process, at least in the early stages of chronicity. The association between perceived preferential treatment and disability is particularly strong for household, recreational, and the more subtle forms of job disability. The author discusses the implications of these findings, and suggests further areas for investigation.

117. Idelson, Roberta K.; Croog, Sydney H.; and Levine, Sol. "Changes in Self-concept During the Year After a First Heart Attack: A Natural History Approach." *American Archives of Rehabilitation Therapy*, 22, 1 and 2 (March and June 1974): 10-20 and 25-31.

This article is based on a longitudinal case study of the recovery process in males who have suffered a primary myocardial infarction. A sample of 11 men and 10 wives were interviewed over a two-year period. Recovery from heart attack is approached as a form of adult socialization. Two basic questions are pursued: "What changes take place in the self-concepts of men who are thrust into the role of chronic heart patient?" and "What factors influence these changes?"

The following stages and their accompanying predominant self-concepts are described: (1) fragile survivor, (2) recovering patient, (3) ambiguity and conflict, (4) normal but different, and (5) a man who once had a heart attack. Tasks and barriers to resocialization are discussed. As self-perception changes, a given sequence of tasks is viewed as moving the socialization process forward. Tasks center on facing reality, experimenting, and reorganizing the psychic image.

118. Janicki, Matthew P. "Attitudes of Health Professionals Toward Twelve Disabilities." *Perceptual and Motor Skills*, 30 (February 1970): 77-78.

54 health professionals were asked to rank 12 disabilities in relation to degree of disturbance to them, with number 1 most disturbing and number 12 least disturbing. The results were as follows: blindness 1st, paraplegia 2nd, amputated arm 3rd, amputated leg 4th, arthritis 5th, asthma 6th, deafness 7th, facial disfiguration 8th, high blood pressure 9th, chronic headaches 10th, diabetes 11th, and stomach ulcers 12th. The author interprets these findings to indicate that disabilities dealing with impairment of motor ability were considered as more disturbing than disabilities dealing with cranial or systemic disorders.

The Studies

119. Jasnos, Theodore M., and Hakmiller, Karl L. "Some Effects of Lesion Level and Emotional Cures on Affective Expression in Spinal Cord Patients." *Psychological Reports*, 37 (1975): 859-870.

    The effect of peripheral sense change on emotional expression in 24 male accident victims who had suffered severe damage to the spinal cord resulting in complete motor and sensory paralysis was assessed. Less intense feelings of arousal were expressed by subjects with higher (cervical) lesions than by subjects with lower (thoracic and lumbar) lesions. Evidence was used by authors to support the Schachterian view that physiological events at the periphery instigate the individual to incorporate environmental information into perception of one's emotional state; significant antecedent of emotional experiences.

120. Jenkins, C.C.; Zyzanski, S.J.; Roseman, R.H.; and Cleveland, G.L. "Association of Coronary-Prone Behavior Scores with Recurrence of Coronary Heart Disease." *Journal of Chronic Diseases*, 24 (1971): 601-611.

    This study investigated the relationship between social-psychological factors (Type A behavior) and recurrence of coronary heart disease. Type A behavior is measured by the Jenkins Activity Survey and characterized by extremes of competitiveness, striving for achievement, impatience, restlessness, and explosiveness of speech. Two samples of men sustaining recurrent myocardial infarction scored significantly higher on Type A behavior than the group of men with only a single incident. The authors argue that test scores can be used to predict patients with potential recurrent cases of chronic heart disease.

121. Johnson, Roger A. "Creative Thinking in the Absence of Language: Deaf Versus Hearing Adolescents." *Child Study Journal*, 7, 2 (Spring 1978): 49-57.

    131 deaf and 131 hearing adolescents aged 11 to 19 were administered the Figural Form B of the Torrance Tests of Creative Thinking (TTCT) to obtain creative thinking scores. The deaf subjects scored significantly higher than the hearing adolescents on the Fluency, Flexibility, and Elaboration Tests of TTCT. Deaf adolescents scored somewhat higher as their ages increased, while there was little increment for the hearing sub-

jects. The sex of the subjects was not significant. The findings of this study are contrary to the widely held view that intellectual development is retarded in the absence of language.

122. Jones, Reginald L. "The Hierarchical Structure of Attitudes Toward the Exceptional." *Exceptional Children*, 39, 6 (March 1974): 430-435.

The structure of atttitudes towards the exceptional was studied using factor analysis. The subjects were 132 female and male college students who completed a 78-item social distance scale. Support for hierarchical structure is presented as attitudes toward the physically handicapped vary from the psychologically disabled as well as the mentally retarded. Findings suggest that mildly mentally retarded are viewed more favorably than severely mentally retarded.

123. Jones, Reginald L. "Correlates of Orthopedically Disabled School Children's School Achievement and Interpersonal Relationship." *Rehabilitation Literature*, 35, 9 (September 1974): 272-275, 288.

The sample consisted of 102 children between the ages of 6 and 16 years who were enrolled in a special elementary school for orthopedically disabled children in a large midwestern city. Findings were as follows:
 (1) There was no relationship between the subject's degree of mobility and locus of control of self-orientation, teacher-rated achievement, or teacher-rated relationship of index subject with other students or teachers.
 (2) There was a positive relationship between degree of mobility and degree of physical disability.
 (3) There was no relationship between type of disability and school achievement.
 (4) There was no relationship between age at disability and other cited variables.

124. Jones, Reginald L., and Siski, D. "Early Perceptions of Orthopedic Disability: A Developmental Study." *Rehabilitation Literature*, 31, 2 (February 1970): 34-38.

The subjects were 230 children enrolled in pre-school and kindergarten classes ranging in age from two to six years. Each subject was presented pictures of children with different kinds of handicaps as

well as a "normal child." Each subject was asked 10
questions about each presented stimuli. The findings
indicated that the perceptions of limitations imposed
by orthopedic disability appear with some consistency
beginning at about age four. Except in one area, the
second finding is that there was no significant difference in the subjects' responses to drawings of disabled and nondisabled children at any age level. The
one exception was that five year olds were less willing
to play with a disabled person.

125. Kaltsounis, B. "Differences in Verbal Creative Thinking
Abilities Between Deaf and Hearing Children." *Psychological Reports*, 26 (1970): 727-733.

351 hearing and 67 deaf children in grades four, five,
and six were administered the Thinking Creatively with
Words Form A. The findings indicated that fluency and
originality scores were dependent upon hearing status
(higher for deaf children), sex, and grade level.
Flexibility scores were independent of these variables.
Findings support the premise of the lack of effect of
deafness on creativity.

126. Kapp, Kathy. "Self Concept of the Cleft Lip or Palate
Child." *Cleft Palate Journal*, 16 (1979): 171-176.

This investigation examined the relationship of the
self-concept of children with cleft lip and/or palate
to the self-concept of children without clefts. 34
children with cleft lip and/or palate between the ages
of 11 and 13 were individually matched with 34 school-
children without clefts. Each child was given the
Piers-Harris Children's Self Concept Scale. Children
with clefts, regardless of sex, reported a significantly greater dissatisfaction with physical appearance. A
significant interaction effect between sex and presence
or absence of cleft was found on three cluster scores,
with cleft girls reporting greater unhappiness and dissatisfaction, less success in school, and more anxiety.

127. Karniski, Marsha A. Perkins. "The Effect of Increased
Knowledge of Body Systems and Function on Attitudes
Toward the Disabled." *Rehabilitation Counseling Bulletin*, 22, 1 (September 1978): 16-20.

This study sought to determine if an increased knowledge of body systems and functioning (handicapped and
nonhandicapped) would affect the personal-space behav-

ior of sixth-grade students on encountering a person who appeared to be disabled. Two sixth-grade classrooms were selected. The experimental group of 20 students received instruction (eight 45-minute lessons) on body systems and functioning, while the 19 students in the control group did not. Personal space was measured by the distance in inches between a wheelchair student and the subjects. Chairs were set at predetermined positions in the room. The findings indicated that the subjects in the experimental group sat closer to the wheelchair students than those in the control group.

128. Kastner, Sheldon. "Tolerance for the Unstable and Defensive Role Adjustment in Response to Sudden Physical Disability." *Journal of Psychology*, 83, 2 (March 1973): 257-262.

This study assesses reactions of 38 males who had suddenly become physically disabled by traumatic injury. Responses to the phi phenomenon were used to determine respondents' cognitive style. The results indicate that subjects tolerant of the unstable are better able to integrate the notions of disabled and nondisabled than intolerant subjects. Thus, personality patterns are viewed as important in determining reaction to sudden disability. Denial of disability may be important in the beginning stages of rehabilitation, but it later becomes necessary to integrate concepts of nondisability with one's concept of disability.

129. Katz, Phyllis A.; Katz, Irwin; and Cohen, Shirley. "White Children's Attitude Toward Blacks and Physically Handicapped: A Developmental Study." *Journal of Educational Psychology*, 68 (1976): 20-24.

80 white elementary school children were tested by either a white or black adult who was or was not seated in a wheelchair. The subjects were asked to make three kinds of ratings concerning the adult: physical distance, imitation, and helping. On all three measures, the white experimenter was favored over the black one, in both the wheelchair and nonwheelchair conditions.

130. Katz, Shlomo, and Shurka, Esther. "The Influence of Contextual Variables on Evaluation of the Physically Disabled by the Nondisabled." *Rehabilitation Literature*, 38, 11-12 (November/December 1977): 369-373.

The Studies 47

226 eleventh-grade Israeli high school students were the subjects for the study. Simulated life history interviews with an amputee, a man with a facial disfigurement, a blind person, a disabled man and a disabled soldier in uniform were presented to the subjects. The subjects were asked to rate each life history in relation to areas of social functioning. Findings were as follows:
(1) Disabled veterans were rated the highest by the subjects.
(2) Disability type was not a significant variable in influencing ratings.

131. Keilbaugh, William S. "Attitudes of Classroom Teachers Toward Their Visually Handicapped Students." *Journal of Visual Impairment and Blindness*, 71, 10 (December 1977): 430-434.

This study presents questionnaire responses of suburban Philadelphia elementary school teachers toward their mainstream, visually handicapped students. Teachers who had previous contact with the visually impaired and those who had previous exposure to special education were somewhat more positive in their attitudes toward the students. Teachers surveyed did not agree as to the standards that visually handicapped students should meet in regular classroom situations.

132. Keith, Robert L.; Ewert, J.C.; and Flowers, C.R. "Factors Influencing the Learning of Esophageal Speech." *British Journal of Disorders of Communication*, 9, 2 (October 1974): 110-116.

This study of 49 male laryngectomized patients was conducted to determine the relationship between mastery of esophageal speech and various age, educational, and psychologic factors. The factors studied were age, education, intelligence, personality indices, and number of speech therapy sessions. Three variables were found to correlate significantly with the final speech proficiency rating: initial speech proficiency rating, depression (Minnesota Multiphasic Personality Inventory Scale 2), and educational level. The results indicate that age and the educational and psychologic variables investigated in this study are not as important to success in learning esophageal speech as indicated by previous authors.

133. Kemp, B.J., and Vash, C.L. "Productivity After Injury in a Sample of Spinal Cord Injured Persons: A Pilot Study." *Journal of Chronic Diseases*, 24 (1971): 259-275.

This study investigated the factors associated with five-years' post-onset adjustment of spinal-cord-injured persons. The sample was composed of 50 individuals. Productivity ratings resulted in five groups ranging from most productive (all persons employed full-time) to least productive (no subject has been employed or attended school since injury). The findings indicated that the individuals associated with greatest productivity were those who (1) reported a high number of goals (forward-looking), (2) paid minimal attention to physical loss, (3) scored significantly higher on creative thinking, and (4) were younger.

134. Kennedy, Patricia, and Bruininks, Robert H. "Social Status of Hearing Impaired Children in Regular Classrooms." *Exceptional Children*, 39, 5 (February 1974): 336-342.

The social status of 15 first- and second-grade students in regular classrooms was assessed by three sociometric scales. There were no significant differences on the three scales between hearing-impaired and non-hearing-impaired children.

135. Kennedy, Patricia; Northcott, Winifred; McCauley, Robert; and Williams, Susan M. "Longitudinal Sociometric and Cross-Sectional Data in Mainstreaming Hearing Impaired Children." *Volta Review*, 78 (February/March 1976): 71-81.

This study examined the peer acceptance and self-perceived status of 11 severe to profoundly deaf pupils enrolled in regular public school elementary classrooms over a three-year period. There were no significant differences between the deaf children and a matched group on the two criterion measures. There were also no significant differences between the two groups on several achievement tests. The authors argue that these findings support early mainstreaming of deaf children.

136. Khan, Aman U.; Herndon, Charles H.; and Ahamdian, Seyed U. "Social and Emotional Adaptations of Children with Transplanted Kidneys and Chronic Hemodialysis." *American Journal of Psychiatry*, 127, 9 (March 1971): 1194-1198.

This is a follow-up of 14 children associated with a kidney transplant project. They had been patients for varying lengths of time and had varying kinds of kidney problems and transplant experiences. Social adjustment, emotional status, level of intelligence, and self-concept were the main characteristics studied. A number of serious social and emotional difficulties were found. Feelings of social isolation, excessive dependency on parents, and depression were common.

137. Kogan, Kate L.; Tyler, Nancy; and Turner, Patricia. "The Process of Interpersonal Adaptation Between Mothers and Their Cerebral Palsied Children." *Developmental Medicine and Child Neurology*, 16, 4 (August 1974): 518-527.

This is a report of an observational study of the interaction between 10 young children with cerebral palsy and their mothers. Observations were conducted on three occasions at ten-month intervals. Sessions between children and their therapists were also observed. Both mothers and therapists decreased their show of affection over time. All mothers decreased their affection, but especially those who had a child who was not making progress in walking. Questions are raised as to how parental reactions are influenced by doctors and other workers as they interact with the child.

138. Kohler, Emmett T., and Graves, William, III. "Factor Analysis of the Disability Factor Scales with the Little Jiffy, Mark III." *Rehabilitation Psychology*, 20, 2 (Summer 1973): 102-107.

Using data obtained from graduate students in a guidance course, this article reports on factor analysis of the Disability Factor Scales. The Amputation, Blindness, and Cosmetic Conditions Scales are analyzed. The use of the scales as a measure of attitude toward the dimensions of net affect, authoritarian virtuousness, distressed identification, and cosmetic aversion is supported.

139. Korsch, Barbara M.; Negrete, Vida F.; Gardner, James E.; Wernstock, Carol L.; Mercer, Ann S.; Grushken, Carl M.; and Fine, Richard N. "Kidney Transplantation in Children: Psycho-Social Follow-up on Child and Family." *Journal of Pediatrics*, 83 (September 1973): 399-408.

55 children treated for kidney diseases by transplantation were compared with a well group of children. There were no significant differences in personality disturbances between the renal sample and the well sample. Those children who did not comply with immunosupportive therapy were the group with the highest rate of personality disturbance. It is this fact, the authors argue, which is an important predictor of emotional problems.

140. Kuhn, Judith. "A Comparison of Teachers' Attitudes Toward Blindness and Exposures to Blind Children." *New Outlook for the Blind*, 65, 10 (December 1971): 337-340.

This study seeks to determine whether regular classroom teachers in a school with facilities of a resource room for blind children would verbally express more positive attitudes toward blindness, as measured by a questionnaire, than teachers without exposure to blind children. The Attitudes to Blindness Scale is used. The two groups of teachers did not differ in attitude. Questions are asked about what activities should supplement exposure if attitudes are to be changed.

141. Lafitte, Jose. "Rehabilitation Potential of Hearing-Impaired Clients." *American Annals of the Deaf*, 123, 5 (August 1978): 580-587.

This study seeks to identify "biographical" variables related to rehabilitation success or failure in hearing-impaired young adults. An attempt is made to develop multivariate predictions. The variables identified as most important to rehabilitation outcome were: previous employment, age, secondary disabilities, race, length of residence in the U.S., primary source of support, mode of communication, and education. Variables contributing least were those associated with degree of hearing loss and onset of disability.

142. Lamb, Marilyn; Wilson, Frank B.; and Leeper, Herbert A. "The Intellectual Function of Cleft Palate Children Compared on the Basis of Cleft Type and Sex." *Cleft Palate Journal*, 10, 4 (October 1973): 367-377.

The sample consisted of 73 children with cleft lip and/or palate between 5 and 16 years of age referred to the Cleft Palate Team of the Jewish Hospital of St. Louis. The findings indicated that there were no cleft type differences when sex of patient was not considered. When sex of patient was considered, females with cleft lip and palate scored significantly lower on the two tests of intellectual function than any other subgroup. Findings suggest that females with cleft lip and palate may be the most vulnerable subgroup of the patient population.

143. LaMendola, Walter F., and Pellegrini, Ronald V. "Quality of Life and Coronary Artery Bypass Surgery Patients." *Social Science and Medicine*, 13A, 4 (June 1979): 457-461.

Through demographic records and interviews, this study reports on 95 patients who underwent coronary bypass surgery at a Pittsburgh hospital. Focus is on quality of life and the operation. Improvement in quality of life is a function of patient's postoperative experiences and perception of his physical limits. The latter is likely to influence desire to return to work. Few patients viewed themselves as physically limited. The researchers attribute this view to satisfaction with outcome of surgery. Retirement and unemployment rates are scrutinized. The researchers move from work status as the main measure of surgery success to a more generalized productivity measure. With stress on affiliative experience, discussion is offered on the conditions which lead to improvement in quality of life following coronary bypass surgery.

144. Langlois, Judith H., and Downs, A. Chris. "Peer Relations as a Function of Physical Attractiveness: The Eye of the Beholder or Behavioral Reality?" *Child Development*, 50 (1979): 409-418.

64 three- and five-year-old boys and girls were selected as subjects on the basis of physical attractiveness. Their behavior in same age and sex dyads which were formed on the basis of physical attractiveness were observed in a play setting. No difference based on attractiveness was observed for three year olds. Unattractive five-year-old children aggressed against peers more often than attractive children. Unattractive five-year-old children were more active than attractive children. No differences in affiliative behavior were associated with attractiveness. Authors argue that these findings do support the notion that differences between attractive and unattractive children

are indeed behavioral realities and do not merely exist
in the eye of the beholder.

145. Langlois, Judith H., and Stephan, Cookie. "The Effects
of Physical Attractiveness and Ethnicity on Children's
Behavior Attributions and Peer Preferences." *Child
Development*, 48, 4 (December 1977): 1964-1968.

Subjects were 120 male and female students who were
in kindergarten and fourth grade. There were an equal
number of black, white, and Mexican-American children.
The stimulus child was rated on behavioral characteristics. Attractive stimulus children were liked more,
were perceived as being smarter and friendlier than
unattractive stimulus children. Physical attractiveness was more important than ethnic status.

146. Lass, Norman J.; Gasperini, Richard M.; Overberger,
James E.; and Connolly, M. Estelle. "The Exposure
of Medical and Dental Students to the Disorder of
Cleft Palate." *Cleft Palate Journal*, 10, 3 (July
1973): 306-311.

A questionnaire study of knowledge about cleft palate
was undertaken with 173 medical students and 199 dental
students at West Virginia University Medical Center.
The findings indicate a deficiency in basic knowledge
of the disorder of cleft palate and its accompanying
associated problems by both groups of students. This
lack of knowledge was associated with the students'
lack of exposure to cleft palate in the classroom and
the clinic.

147. Lavine, Molly B. "An Exploratory Study of the Sibships
of Blind Children." *Journal of Visual Impairment and
Blindness*, 71, 3 (March 1977): 102-107.

Five preschool white children blind from birth and
their sighted siblings are subjects for this study.
The first four years of life are explored. Findings
suggest that the sibship development of blind children
is the same as sighted children, that sibship offers
the blind child an opportunity to adapt to blindness
and learn general coping skills and that family expectations, particularly mother-child expectations, that
may be acted out in sibship interaction impact on the
blind child's readiness for school.

148. Lazar, A.L.; Gensley, J.T.; and Orpet, R.E. "Changing
Attitudes of Young Mentally Gifted Children Toward

Handicapped Persons." *Exceptional Children*, 37, 8 (April 1971): 600-602.

The purpose of this study was to determine if the attitudes of a group of young mentally gifted children could be influenced in terms of greater understanding and acceptance of handicapped persons as the result of a special instructional program presented by their workshop teacher. Two groups of young mentally gifted children, matched for IQ and CA, were selected for the study. It was found that the group exposed to the special instructional program was influenced to favorably change their attitudes toward handicapped people.

149. Lazar, Alfred; Orpet, Russell; and Demos, George. "The Impact of Class Instruction on Changing Students Attitudes." *Rehabilitation Counseling Bulletin*, 20, 1 (September 1976): 66-68.

This study ascertained whether attitudes of college students toward the physically disabled could be changed in a favorable direction. Class instruction consisted of a three-hour period of instruction for students enrolled in a special class. The attitudes were measured by the Attitude Toward Disabled Persons Scale. The findings indicated that the post-test scores were significantly higher for the college students, especially the male students.

150. Lazar, Alfred L.; Stodden, Robert; and Sullivan, Neil V. "A Comparison of Attitudes Held by Male and Female Future School Administrators Toward Instructional Goals, Personal Adjustment, and the Handicapped." *Rehabilitation Literature*, 37, 7 (July 1976): 198-201.

17 females and 34 males, ranging in age from 24 to 52 years, who were students in advance administration, were the subjects for this study. On three different measures of attitudes, there was no statistically significant difference between the male and female subjects.

151. Lazar, A.L.; Demos, G.D.; Gaines, L.; Rogers, D.; and Stirnkorb, M. "Attitudes of Handicapped and Nonhandicapped University Students on Three Attitude Scales." *Rehabilitation Literature*, 38, 2 (February 1978): 49-52.

The results of the study indicated that the handicapped and nonhandicapped did not differ in their social adjustment or in their attitude toward handicapped individuals. They did differ in terms of instructional goals, with the handicapped being more cognitively inclined than nonhandicapped.

152. Lehon, Lester. "The Relationship Between Intelligence and the Mastery of Mobility Skills Among Blind Persons." *New Outlook for the Blind*, 66, 4 (April 1972): 115-119.

Mobility skills are necessary for blind persons to be able to travel from one place to another. This study compares three groups of blind persons, the above average, the average, and the below average in intelligence. Subjects with less than average intelligence acquired mobility skills at a significantly slower rate than subjects with above average intelligence. The level of mobility-skill achievement was not a function of intelligence.

153. Levine, Jacob, and Ziegler, Edward. "Denial and Self-Image in Stroke, Lung Cancer, and Heart Disease Patients." *Journal of Counseling and Clinical Psychology*, 43, 6 (December 1975): 751-757.

Patients with stroke, lung cancer, and heart disease were asked to compare their real versus ideal selves for the present time and "about a year ago." There was also a control group. All three patient groups employed denial as measured by little difference in real and ideal self between time periods. Order of denial from highest to lowest was: stroke, lung cancer, heart disease. The functions of denial are discussed in terms of protecting the patient from frustration and despair.

154. Levitin, Theresa E. "Deviants as Active Participants in the Labeling Process: The Visibly Handicapped." *Social Problems*, 22, 4 (April 1975): 548-557.

Using unstructured interviews with adults who had recently become handicapped through accident or illness, this study notes how choice about a deviant identity is related to duration of the deviance-handicap and the social context to the labeling process. The encounters stressed are sociable encounters and encounters with control agents--physical therapists.

155. Levitt, Eugene A.; Rosenbaum, Arthur L.; Willerman, Lee; and Levitt, Marc. "Intelligence of Retinoblas-

toma Patients and their Siblings." *Child Development*, 43, 3 (September 1972): 939-948.

Sighted and blind retinoblastoma patients were compared with their normal siblings on standardized tests of intelligence. Unilaterally affected patients were compared with bilaterally affected patients, as well as those patients blinded by the disease. Unilaterally affected patients did not differ from their controls. Bilaterally affected patients were inferior to their controls, whereas those patients who were blinded by the disease were superior to their controls. The primary conclusion was that retinoblastoma per se is not associated with intellectual performance.

156. Lewis, Ruth. "Survey of the Intelligence of Cleft Lip and Cleft Palate Children in Ontario." *British Journal of Disorders in Communication*, 6 (April 1971): 17-25.

548 children with cleft lip and cleft palate, ranging in age from 4 to 16 years at the time of testing, were assessed in relation to IQ as measured by the Stanford-Binet Intelligence Scale Form. The control group consisted of 50 patients' siblings who were compared with 50 patients. Findings indicated that when compared to the norm, IQ's of patients with cleft lip and cleft palate were significantly lower. IQ's of patients with cleft lip and cleft palate were significantly lower than for siblings. From these findings, author argues that the anomaly itself, rather than type of family, is the key variable in determining the patient's IQ.

157. Liljefors, I., and Rahe, R.H. "An Identical Twin Study of Psycho-social Factors in Coronary Heart Disease in Sweden." *Psychosomatic Medicine*, 32 (September/October 1970): 523-542.

32 pairs of Swedish identical male twins, 42 to 67 years of age, who were discordant for coronary heart disease (CHD), were analyzed. In relation to work, lack of leisure, home problems and life dissatisfactions, the CHD group was significantly different from their less CHD-afflicted brothers. The life dissatisfaction category provided the most significant correlation with CHD severity. No significant differences between a subject's medical history and physical examination data and the occurrence of CHD were noted.

158. Linkowski, Donald C., and Dunn, Marilyn A. "Self-Concept and Acceptance of Disability." *Rehabilitation Counseling Bulletin*, 18, 1 (September 1974): 28-32.

Data was collected from 55 college students with physical disabilities to assess the relationship between self-concept and acceptance of disability. Self-concept was assessed by a Self-Ideal Q Sort and Satisfaction with Social Relationships Scale; while acceptance of disability was measured by the Acceptance of Disability Scale. Significant positive correlations were found among the three scales.

159. Lugar, Owen, and Kelz, James W. "The Vocational Rehabilitation of Stroke Victims: Description and Prediction." *Rehabilitation Counseling Bulletin*, 14, 4 (June 1971): 201-212.

The purpose of this study was to identify variables that would predict who will be a potentially successful rehabilitated patient (CVA). Demographic variables were socioeconomic status (over $3,000 income), spouse's employment status prior to and after acceptance (employed), and Social Security Disability Insurance status at referral and acceptance (nonapplicant). Medical variables included sex (female), upper extremity (flaccid extremity), and ambulatory status (ambulatory). Scale did predict correctly 74% or 168 of 227 patients outcome of rehabilitation status.

160. Macdougall, J.C., and Morin, S. "Sexual Attitudes and Self-Reported Behavior of Congenitally Disabled Adults." *Canadian Journal of Behavioral Science*, 11, 3 (July 1979): 189-204.

This is an interview-based study of the sexual behavior of congenitally disabled adults aged 18 to 35. The group expressed liberal attitudes towards sexuality, but not great personal interest. Most subjects were unmarried; more than half had never had a serious intimate relationship with the opposite sex; many seemed uninformed about sexual matters. The researchers attributed negative attitudes toward sex to restrictive living conditions and insufficient sex education and guidance.

161. Macguggie, Robert A.; Jorgensen, Gary Q.; and Janzen, Frederick V. "Need for Approval and Counseling Outcomes." *Personnel and Guidance Journal*, 48, 8 (April 1970): 653-656.

The purpose of this study was to ascertain the effects of the client's need for approval on the outcome of counseling. The Marlowe-Crowne Social Desirability Scale was administered to 167 applicants at a state rehabilitation agency after the initial interview. The 88 successfully rehabilitated patients scored significantly higher on this scale than did the 79 nonrehabilitated patients. There were no significant differences between the two groups in relation to age, sex, marital status, educational attainment, source of referral, work history, age at disablement, and characteristics of major disabling condition. Findings support the premise that high need for approval may be an asset in obtaining work.

162. Magyar, Charles W.; Nystrom, John B.; and Johansen, Norma. "A Follow-Up Study of Former Cerebral Palsied Students at a School for Neuro-Orthopedically Disabled Children." *Rehabilitation Literature*, 38, 2 (February 1977): 40-42.

48 students who were 18 years of age and older as of January 1, 1976 and who had attended Lakeview completed a follow-up questionnaire. The 48 represented a 62% returned rate. The sample was divided into employed, nonproductive, and student groups. Findings were as follows:
   (1) The employed group was more likely to have a high school diploma.
   (2) The employed group was more mobile than the nonproductive and student groups.
   (3) The employed group was the only group in which persons were married and had children.
   (4) The employed group was more likely to attend church regularly.
   (5) There was no significant difference between the the three groups of subjects in relation to IQ.

163. Mallenby, Terry W. "The Effects of Extended Contact with 'Normals' on the Social Behavior of Hard of Hearing Children." *Journal of Social Psychology*, 95, 1 (February 1975): 137-138.

This research examines interaction patterns and social behavior among three groups of children: hard-of-hearing children who transferred from an institution to a normal public school setting, hard-of-hearing children from an institutional setting, and normal hearing children. The hard-of-hearing children who attended the institution stood farther away from the normal hearing children and exhibited more flight reaction to intrusion and physical rejection than either the normal hearing children or the hard-of-hearing children who attended the normal public school. The study suggests that prolonged interaction with normal hearing children might influence the social behavior of hard-of-hearing children and might enhance self-acceptance.

164. Malone, Russell L.; Ptacek, Paul; and Malone, Marquette S. "Attitudes Expressed by Families of Aphasics." *British Journal of Disorders of Communication*, 5 (October 1970): 174-179.

10 husbands and 20 wives of persons with aphasia were administered the Boles Scale to assess their attitudes to aphasics. The onset of aphasia ranged from six months to three years prior to testing. Language disability of the patients ranged from mild to extremely severe, with most of the patients demonstrating moderately severe impairment. No patient was expected to achieve "normal" language or ambulation.

The findings indicated that most spouses of patients with aphasia have negative attitudes in the following areas: retributive guilt, unrealistic attitudes, rejection, overprotection, and social withdrawal. The findings suggest that the spouses need (1) more accurate information about aphasia, and (2) counseling regarding their attitudes and feelings.

165. Manaster, Al. "The Theragnostic Group in a Rehabilitation Center for Visually Handicapped Persons." *New Outlook for the Blind*, 65, 8 (October 1971): 261-264.

This article reports on the use of "T" groups at the Illinois Institute for the Blind. The groups were introduced to help relieve stress experienced by new or potential clients during an evaluation period. The researcher reports that the evaluees were able to develop more positive feelings about themselves and others in relation to their disability, to the rehabilitation center, and to the future. Interaction in the "T" group provided both participants and institute with insights into personality dynamics and the potentials of the visually handicapped for participation in the total rehabilitation program. The researcher feels that discovery of worth as a human being by the evaluee, rather than merely being an object to be evaluated, is the most important benefit.

166. Manaster, Al, and Kucharis, Sue. "Experimental Methods in Group Counseling Program with Blind Children." *New Outlook for the Blind*, 66, 1 (January 1972): 15-18.

This study reports the results of group counseling sessions that were part of a summer mobility program at the Illinois Visually Handicapped Institute. Goals were: to enable the youngsters aged 11 to 18 to develop mobility skills, to add proficiency to their daily living activities, and to increase their personal and social skills. The report described the experiential techniques and methods used. The blind adolescents reportedly confronted their own feelings and made better progress than students not exposed to the experiential methods. The authors attribute the progress to the adolescents' feelings of being involved and the fact that the sessions afforded them an opportunity to do and say things they otherwise would not have been allowed to experience.

167. Marinelli, Robert P., and Kelz, James W. "Anxiety and Attitudes Toward Visibly Disabled Persons." *Rehabilitation Counseling Bulletin*, 16, 4 (June 1973): 198-205.

108 undergraduate rehabilitation education students comprised the sample for this study. The measures employed were the Attitude Toward Disabled Person Scale, Manifest Anxiety Scale, and a heartbeat monitoring (state anxiety). The latter was used during a standardized interaction between the subject and a cosmetically disabled patient. Findings indicated that negative attitudes toward disabled persons are positively associated with more state and trait anxiety. The converse was also true.

168. Markides, A. "Home Atmosphere and Linguistics Progress of Pre-School Hearing-Handicapped Children." *Teacher of the Deaf*, 70, 11 (January 1972): 7-13.

This study compares the linguistic progress of two groups of hearing-handicapped children. Group A consisted of 19 children from secure homes; Group B consisted of 16 children from homes with various social and emotional problems. Children in Group A made significantly better linguistic progress than those children in Group B. The author argues for more social work intervention with families similar to those in

Group B. Such intervention might allow those families to benefit better from the guidance provided by the teacher of the deaf.

169. Markson, E.W. "Patient Semeiology of a Chronic Disease: Rheumatoid Arthritis." *Social Science and Medicine*, 5, 2 (June 1971): 159-167.

   This paper focuses on the semeiology developed by a group of 46 women with rheumatoid arthritis. Specifically, it describes some techniques of medical management employed by the patients, their etiological explanations of the disease, how they limit their behavior and manage role expectations, and their view of themselves.

170. Martin, Helen L. "Parents' and Children's Reactions to Burns and Scalds in Children." *British Journal of Medical Psychology*, 43, 2 (June 1970): 183-192.

   Through a series of interviews with child burn victims and their parents, this study suggests the behavior of burned and scalded children is closely related to disturbances in mothering behavior, resulting from the injury and its treatment, and the way the mother assigns responsibility for the injury. Mothers' need to mother burn victims is discussed.

171. Martin, P. "Marital Breakdown in Families of Patients with Spina Bifida Cystica." *Developmental Medicine and Child Neurology*, 17, 6 (December 1975): 757-764.

   In this study of families of children with spina bifida cystica it was found that divorce or separation of the parents did not occur significantly more frequently than in the general population of the U.S. While in some cases a child with spina bifida cystica may be the factor responsible for the breakdown of a marriage that is already strained, in other cases such a child may bring the parents closer together.
   A further finding was that, compared with other children in this study, a greater proportion of children with spina bifida cystica did not remain with their natural parents. These observations stress the importance of early evaluation of a family with a child with spina bifida cystica, and the need for assistance for both natural and adoptive parents.

172. Mathes, Eugene W. "The Effects of Physical Attractiveness and Anxiety on Heterosexual Attraction over a

Series of Five Encounters." *Journal of Marriage and the Family*, 37, 4 (November 1975): 769-773.

26 college student couples who had five dates rated their partners on physical attractiveness, and completed the Taylor Manifest Anxiety Scale. Physically attractive students were better liked than unattractive students over the five dates. The same findings for anxious students for first dating encounter also was found. From a rational perspective, the author concludes that the first finding supports irrationality, while the latter one supports rationality.

173. Mathews, Karen A. "Efforts to Control by Children and Adults with the Type A Coronary-Prone Behavior Pattern." *Child Development*, 50 (1979): 842-847.

The present study examined the initial reactions of Type A and Type B boys and men to uncontrollable events. Type A coronary-prone behavior pattern is characterized by competitiveness, aggressiveness, and impatience, and is hypothesized to be associated with maintaining and asserting control over uncontrollable events. 152 subjects, 76 Type A and 76 Type B individuals, comprised the sample. Findings indicated that Type A responded initially to highly salient, uncontrollable events with more vigorous efforts to assert control than Type B. This finding held for both the boys and the men. The author argues the support of the premise that the basis for adult heart attacks lies with early childhood behavior patterns.

174. Matovu, H.L. "Changing Community Attitudes Towards Epilepsy in Uganda." *Social Science and Medicine*, 8, 1 (January 1974): 47-50.

This is an experiment with the use of two health education methods, lecture-discussion versus written, to change attitudes toward epilepsy. Using a pre- and post-test questionnaire, the researcher found that both methods produced improvement in knowledge among village and school groups. The lecture-discussion method was slightly more effective. The importance of this research rests in the fact that it demonstrates that even in low literacy areas, written materials can be used successfully to change attitudes. Also, it affirms an attitude change process whereby change can be initiated by identifying literate individuals in the group to act as change agents.

175. Matson, Ronald R., and Brooks, Nancy A. "Adjusting to Multiple Sclerosis: An Exploratory Study." *Social Science and Medicine*, 11, 4 (March 1977): 242-250.

This study examines 174 multiple sclerosis patients on a number of demographic, health related, and adjustment variables. Emphasis is on self-concept as a key to adjustment. Patients did not differ from a non-multiple sclerosis control group in terms of self-concept. They were relatively positive. Steps and processes in adjustment are discussed.

176. Mayadas, Nazneen S. "Houseparents' Expectations: A Crucial Variable in the Performance of Blind Institutionalized Children." *New Outlook for the Blind*, 69, 2 (February 1975): 77-83.

For institutionalized children, houseparents can be "significant others." This study investigates the influence of houseparents on the behavior of institutionalized blind children. Social and instrumental task performance is evaluated. The houseparents emerged as important influences. In this study the houseparents were women. The expectations of houseparents differed from the child's expectations for self. This highlights the modeling by sightless children of sighted individuals.

177. Mayadas, Nazneen S., and Duehn, Wayne D. "The Impact of Significant Adults' Expectations on the Life Style of Visually Impaired Children." *New Outlook for the Blind*, 70, 7 (September 1976): 286-290.

The behavior performance of blind persons is evaluated in terms of role expectations of significant others--counselors, parents, and houseparents. The results suggest a correlation between significant others' expectations and behavior of the blind. Exceptions did occur. The researchers attribute these to social norms and the individual's self-expectation.

178. Mayou, Richard. "The Course and Determinants of Reactions to Myocardial Infarction." *British Journal of Psychiatry*, 134 (June 1979): 588-594.

Data reported were derived from 100 patients and spouses who were interviewed two and twelve months after the first myocardial infarction. The study suggests that global measures of social outcome are misleading and therefore variables such as work, leisure, marriage and family relationships, sex and compliance should be examined separately. The study notes that it is possible to identify individual reaction patterns and that there is continuity in these patterns throughout the convalescent period. Outcomes for spouses can be described and understood similarly to patients' outcomes. The study has implications for understanding response to physical illnesses.

179. McAndrew, I. "Adolescents and Young People with Spina Bifida." *Developmental Medicine and Child Neurology*, 21, 5 (October 1979): 619-629.

Interviews were conducted with 35 adolescents and young people with myelomeningocele. They reported physical problems similar to other persons who suffer from congenital physical disabilities, but also complications not specific to other orthopedic disabilities, e.g., neurogenic bowel and bladder. These problems lead to social embarrassment due to management problems and incontinence. Social esteem is hypothesized to erode as physical disability worsens. It is suggested that ability to cope with physical and emotional problems is not determined by disability but is a product of overall support systems from birth onward.

180. McBroom, William H. "Illness, Illness Behavior and Socioeconomic Status." *Journal of Health and Social Behavior*, 11, 4 (December 1970): 319-326.

A sample of applicants for disability benefits was used in this study to explore the relationship between socioeconomic status and illness. The author sought support of his hypotheses: (1) that illness level varies by status and (2) that subjective responses about illness vary by status. Data obtained from a randomly selected sample drawn from three regions of the U.S. (metropolitan areas of New Orleans and Minneapolis-St. Paul, and the 20 counties contiguous to Columbus, Ohio) did not indicate any substantial linear association for either hypothesis. However, there was a slight positive association between socioeconomic status and indicators of both self-perceived functional and self-perceived social limitations.

181. McGuinness, Richard Michael. "A Descriptive Study of Blind Children Educated in the Itinerant Teacher,

Resource Room, and Special School Settings." *American Foundation for the Blind Research Bulletin*, 20 (March 1970): 1-47.

This is a study of 97 totally blind elementary school children, all of whom had been educated exclusively in either the itinerant teacher, resource room, or special school setting. The Stanford Achievement Subtests of Braille Reading and Word Meaning, Vineland Social Maturity Scale, the Locus of Control Test, and sociometric devices were administered. The results support integrated settings of education for blind children. The itinerant teacher and resource room settings facilitated the social integration of blind children with their sighted peers, and promoted social maturity and independence, without sacrificing Braille skills.

182. McKelvre, Stuart J., and Matthews, Sharon J. "Effects of Physical Attractiveness and Favorableness of Character on Liking." *Psychological Reports*, 38 (1976): 1223-1230.

40 subjects gave ratings of liking a person for photographs of 24 females who were physically attractive or unattractive and who were described as having a favorable or unfavorable behavior. Both variables contributed significantly to the ratings of liking, although behavior had a stronger effect. Sex differences were also noted with males more influenced by attractiveness, whereas females were more influenced by behavior. The authors conclude that their findings can be accounted for by a general reward theory of interpersonal attraction.

183. McWilliams, Betty Jane, and Matthews, Hannah P. "A Comparison of Intelligence and Social Maturity in Children with Unilateral Complete Clefts and Those with Isolated Cleft Palates." *Cleft Palate Journal*, 16 (1979): 363-372.

This study compared the intelligence and social maturity of four groups of subjects with oralfacial clefts; 111 unilateral complete clefts of the lip and palate; 16 unilateral complete clefts of the lip and palate with associated congenital malformations; 76 clefts of the palate only; and 39 clefts of the palate with associated congenital malformations (n = 39). Comparisons among groups suggested that the subjects in the unilateral cleft lip and palate group were the most competent both mentally and socially, followed by those in the palatal only group. The presence of congenital abnormalities, other than cleft, increased the risk of developmental delays, particularly in subjects with isolated palatal clefts.

184. McWilliams, Betty Jane, and Musgrave, Ross H. "Psychological Implications of Articulation Disorders in Cleft Palate Children." *Cleft Palate Journal*, 9, 4 (October 1972): 294-303.

Three groups of children with different articulation patterns were studied. The mothers reported *more* behavioral symptoms for the children with normal voice quality and articulation errors as compared to those with normal voices. Specific behavioral symptoms were bed wetting and having bad tempers. Children with hypernasal speech were reported to have more behavioral symptoms than normal children. No specific behavioral patterns were noted.

185. McWilliams, Betty Jane, and Paradise, Leone P. "Educational, Occupational and Marital Status of Cleft Palate Adults." *Cleft Palate Journal*, 10, 3 (July 1973): 223-229.

The subjects for the study were 115 patients who had been treated at the University of Pittsburgh Cleft Palate Center. The ages ranged from 18 to 38 with a mean of 24 years. The findings were as follows:
(1) There were no significant differences between the two groups in relation to level of education attained and occupational levels achieved.
(2) There was a significantly larger number of patients with cleft palate who remained single in comparison to their nearest age sibling.

186. Menapace, Robert H., and Lana, Robert H. "Physical Rehabilitation and Attitudes of CVA and Pulmonary Patients." *Psychological Reports*, 28 (1971): 763-768.

28 cerebral-vascular accident (CVA) in-patients and 28 pulmonary out-patients were examined for attitudes toward self and hospital procedure and personnel. Before and after attitude testing occurred six weeks apart. Major findings were as follows:
(1) The self-perception gain scores were higher for CVA patients than for pulmonary patients.

(2) The CVA in-patients became more skeptical than pulmonary patients about hospital procedure and personnel.

187. Merrill, Robert E. "Prognosis for Children with Multiple Handicaps." *American Journal of Diseases of Children*, 121, 3 (March 1971): 207-212.

This is a report on 32 multiply handicapped persons who were patients at the University of Virginia Pediatric Clinic. All 32 discontinued activity in the clinic due to death, or because they reached an age which suggested that medical supervision was more appropriate in a clinic for adults. Data on the patients are summarized. Present status of living patients is reviewed and prognosis estimated. It is postulated that failure may be due to a lack of medical knowledge, poor environment, or a combination of organic and psychological problems. Successful rehabilitation depends on good follow-up and effective school and vocational planning.

188. Mignone, R.J.; Donnelly, E.F.; and Sadowsky, D. "Psychological and Neurological Comparisons of Psychomotor and Non-Psychomotor Epileptic Patients." *Epilepsia*, 11 (1970): 345-359.

98 patients with psychomotor epilepsy were compared with 53 non-psychomotor epilepsy patients. In both groups the sample was 15 years or older, had no evidence of mental retardation or central nervous system involvement other than seizures, and no significant medical or surgical illness or handicap. The findings indicated that there were no significant differences between the two groups in relation to Minnesota Multiphasic Personality Inventory scores and clinical psychiatric profiles. There was no significant difference between the two groups in relation to neurological analysis. The entire epileptic sample was significantly different on the MMPI from a control college student group, and the clinical psychiatric data differed from expected random occurrence.

189. Miller, Ralph H., and Keith, Robert Allen. "Behavioral Mapping in a Rehabilitation Hospital." *Rehabilitation Psychology*, 20, 4 (Winter 1973): 148-155.

The purpose of this article is to demonstrate the utility of a device from environmental psychology, behavioral mapping, for the understanding of hospital behavior. The hourly location and activities of patients in a rehabilitation hospital were charted over time. Findings included: patients spent more time in their rooms than in treatment activities; patients spent more time in socializing or alone than in treatment; treatment took place sporadically during the day, showing marked rises at some time intervals and marked falls at others; on weekends, patients were more often alone as opposed to socializing or being in treatment. Implications of the findings are to question the amount of time a patient should spend in treatment and also indicate that patients are not highly integrated into the social structure of the rehabilitation hospital.

190. Minde, Klaus. "Coping Styles of 34 Adolescents with Cerebral Palsy." *American Journal of Psychiatry*, 135, 11 (November 1978): 1344-1349.

This is a follow-up study of children with cerebral palsy between the ages of 10 to 14. This age period was highlighted by increased awareness of the permanence of handicap, a search for personal and occupational identity, and a desire for withdrawal of parental emotional support.

191. Minde, Klaus K.; Hackett, J.D.; Killou, D.; and Silver, S. "How They Grow Up: 41 Physically Handicapped Children and Their Families." *American Journal of Psychiatry*, 128, 12 (June 1972): 1554-1559.

Development data on 41 crippled children admitted to the MacKay Center in Montreal over a 3- to 4-year period is analyzed. Between the ages of 5 and 9, development was highlighted by: (1) realization that the handicap would not suddenly disappear, (2) leading to severe depression, and (3) hesitant, but gradual readiness to see the condition as part of child's self. Parents' development was most characterized by a struggle between the wish to have a normal child and knowledge of the child's handicap.

192. Mitchell, R.G., and Davison, B. "Educational and Social Characteristics of Children with Asthma." *Archives of Disease in Childhood*, 48 (1973): 467-471.

Asthma was found to affect five percent of the children aged 10 to 15 years in Aberdeen. Severe asthma was associated with semi- and unskilled manual working families. Children with severe asthma tended to come from larger families, regardless of social class. Severe asthma may be overrepresented in lower classes as families in upper classes are able to seek treatment early, preventing the evolvement of severe asthma.

193. Moen, Joan L.; Wilcox, Robert D.; and Burns, Ivan K. "PKU as a Factor in the Development of Self-Esteem." *Journal of Pediatrics*, 90 (June 1977): 1027-29.

The self-esteem of 10 children with PKU was compared with that of seven unaffected siblings. The subjects ranged in ages from 8 to 15 years. The children with PKU had lower self-esteem than their comparison group when measured by the Cooper-Smith Self-Esteem Inventory.

194. Monteiro, Lois A. "After Heart Attack: Behavioral Expectations for the Cardiac." *Social Science and Medicine*, 7, 9 (September 1973): 555-565.

In the assumption of the sick role, and in cardiac rehabilitation programs, patients are urged to return to normal activity levels, within limits of residual heart damage, and at an early time. This study of 1,137 adults in a sample of Rhode Island households describes the image of appropriate behavior for the cardiac held by laypersons.

Respondents favored activity for the cardiac and rejected the passive role. Personal experience with heart disease affected response. Persons who reported having had a heart attack were more favorable to activity restriction. Respondents with higher income and education were more encouraging of activity. Age was negatively associated with a view favoring activity. The author reports consistency of responses with expectations for self were the respondent to have a heart attack.

195. Montgomery, George, and Miller, John. "Assessment and Preparation of Deaf Adolescents for Employment." *British Association of Teachers of the Deaf*, 1, 5 (September 1977): 167-176.

This paper reports on the assessment of deaf adolescents for technical training and employment. It employs previous research findings, the researchers' experiences, and data from two surveys of employment of the deaf in the British Isles. Focus is on the interaction of the total educational, rehabilitation, occupational, and social setting rather than assessment routines at the time of school leaving. The article attempts to give advice to those involved in educational and career development. Special emphasis is given to the development of self-identity in these processes.

196. Morgan, Essie; Hohman, George W.; and Davis, John E., Jr. "Psychosocial Rehabilitation in VA Spinal Cord Injury Centers." *Rehabilitation Psychology*, 21, 1 (Spring 1974): 3-33.

This study reports on the psychosocial rehabilitation process within the Veterans Administration Spinal Cord Injury Center system. Factors reported include: patients' perception of the SCI centers as deficient in physical, psychosocial, and vocational rehabilitation programs; normative social experiences and opportunities to relearn skills necessary for integration into the community were lacking; staffing was inadequate; existing staff were perceived as insensitive to patient needs outside the center. Strong feelings centered around whether the patients were to be "good patients" or productive individuals outside the center setting. Patients wanted to be more self-sufficient and better prepared for outside living. In general the study documents that the centers had moved away from comprehensive rehabilitation and needed to reexamine procedures and purposes.

197. Morin, Stephan F., and Jones, Reginald L. "Social Comparison of Abilities in Blind Children and Adolescents." *Journal of Psychology*, 87, 2 (July 1974): 237-243.

Using structured interviews with 45 blind school-age children, this research tests Festinger's theory of social comparison that predicts that individuals choose one similar to oneself for comparison of abilities. The research supports this theory particularly as sightedness (relevance) and difficulty enter into the task.

198. Mowrer, Donald, E.; Wahl, Priscilla; and Doolan, Susan J. "Effect of Lisping on Audience Evaluation of Male Speakers." *Journal of Speech and Hearing Disorders*, 43, 2 (May 1978): 140-148.

The social consequences of 140 adult listeners' first impressions of lisping were evaluated. Five adult speakers were rated by adult listeners with regard to speaking ability, intelligence, education, masculinity, and friendship. The findings indicated that the evaluators rated adult speakers who lisp lower than non-lispers on all five categories investigated. These findings suggest that efforts to correct lisping are justifiable.

199. Muhlenkamp, A.F. "Attitudes of Nursing Students Toward Eight Major Disabilities." *Psychological Reports*, 29 (1971): 973-974.

34 nursing students ranked eight disabilities according to the degree of difficulty they felt they would experience, were they personally to incur the disability. Findings were as follows: (1) complete blindness; (2) incurable heart condition; (3) incurable TB; (4) complete deafness; (5) migraine headaches; (6) amputated leg (above the knee); (7) incurable ulcerated stomach; (8) amputated arm (above the elbow). Reason for choices fell into four categories: coping vs. succumbing; nonfatal vs. fatal; nonisolating vs. isolating; and normal vs. abnormal.

200. Myers, Beverly A.; Friedman, Stanford B.; and Weiner, Irving B. "Coping with a Chronic Disability: Psychosocial Observations of Girls with Scoliosis Treated with the Milwaukee Brace." *American Journal of Diseases of Children*, 120, 3 (September 1970): 175-181.

26 girls and their mothers were interviewed concerning adjustment to wearing a Milwaukee Brace for scoliosis. Factors aiding coping included intellectual understanding of scoliosis and bracing, optimistic view of outcome, active decision to wear brace, and support of family and medical staff. Negative factors included poor intellectual understanding, denial of conformity, conflicts between mother and daughter, family problems, and long duration for the brace.

201. Nagi, Saad Z. "Epidemiology of Disability Among Adults in the United States." *Milbank Memorial Fund Quarterly*, 54, 4 (Fall 1976): 439-468.

This is a report of an interview survey of a probability sample of 6,493 persons, 18 years of age and over. Indices were utilized for two dimensions of performance (physical and emotional) and of disability (work and independent living). Analysis showed the relative contribution of pathology and impairment to the levels of physical and emotional performance. The author accounted for 38% of the variance in work disability and 74% of dependence-independence in community living through the influence of levels of performance, health conditions, and the four social-demographic conditions of: education, age, sex, and race. The study demonstrates the independence in variance for the indices of disability, limitations in physical and emotional performance, and health conditions of the respondents. They are separate distinct concepts, e.g., impairment is not disability. The study noted the influence of environment in work disability and consistency of data with 1970 census information.

202. Naismith, Lorna D.; Robinson, John F.; Shaw, Gavin B.; and Macintyre, Mary M.J. "Psychological Rehabilitation after Myocardial Infarction." *British Medical Journal*, 1, 6161 (February 17, 1979): 439-442.

Men who had recently had a myocardial infarction were randomly assigned to either a group receiving intensive rehabilitation or to a control group. Outcomes were examined after six months. Neurotic, introverted patients did poorly in the control group, but responded to the experimentation. All patients with a negative attitude towards their illness and prognosis did poorly; those patients with positive attitudes did well. Patients felt that psychological rehabilitation forms a major component of after-myocardial care.

203. Neel, Ann F. "Social and Biological Factors in Child Development." *Psychological Reports*, 40 (1977): 1143-1146.

Groups of 84 healthy black and 49 healthy white, 134 chronically ill black and 17 chronically ill white persons were administered the WISC, Bender-Gestalt, Thematic Appreciation Test, and a figure-drawing test. The chronically ill black group was children with sickle cell anemia. No description was provided for the chronically ill white group. Groups were matched for age, sex, and social class. Findings were as follows: (1) Chronically ill black children scored lowest on all dimensions. (2) Class status had a marked effect on test scores.

The author argues that the findings support the premise that racial differences are in effect health and class differences.

204. Nelson, Marian, and Griner, Gene Gary. "Self-Esteem and Body Image Conception in Paraplegics." *Rehabilitation Counseling Bulletin*, 22, 2 (December 1978): 108-113.

Paraplegics, hospitalized tuberculous patients, and nonhospitalized normal people were compared with three measures to ascertain the relationship between body image and self-concept. The first group consisted of hospitalized spinal cord-injury patients; the second group comprised hospitalized tuberculous patients; and the third group was the control group (nonhospitalized disabled group). Each group had 14 participants and the patient groups were from the Long Beach, California, Veterans Administration Hospital. The measuring instruments were Cattell's Sixteen Personality Factor Questionnaire, The Way I See Myself, and The Draw-A-Person. There were no significant differences among the three groups on the three measures employed. One explanation of the results is that self-concept is a function of numerous variables, of which physical disability is only one.

205. Newman, Joseph. "Faculty Attitudes Toward Handicapped Students." *Rehabilitation Literature*, 37, 7 (July 1976): 194-197.

465 or 57% of the faculty of the University of Pittsburgh completed a survey questionnaire. Findings were as follows:
  (1) 98% of the respondents were in favor of admitting handicapped students, at least on a restricted basis.
  (2) Blindness and deafness were the two sensory handicaps that were perceived as being the most restricted in relation to admission.

206. Nickerson, Eileen T. "Some Correlates of Adjustment by Paraplegics." *Perceptual and Motor Skills*, 32 (February 1971): 11-23.

48 male paraplegic patients of a Veterans Administration hospital were studied to assess adjustment to their physically immobilized disability which involves the loss of ability to walk, feel sensation, to pro-

create, and the control of bowel and bladder function. The subjects' adjustment to the hospital was rated by four hospital staff members on a nine-point, Q-Sort rating scale. The better adjusted group were more likely to be higher educated and had higher occupational attainments prior to their disability. The author argues that the findings do not support the significance of psychological factors but rather the importance of socioeconomic factors for successful coping.

207. Olshansky, Simon, and Beach, Dorothy. "Follow-Up of Clients Placed into Regular Employment." *Rehabilitation Literature*, 35, 8 (August 1974): 237-238.

Telephone interviews were conducted in August 1973 with 237 graduates of a community workshop who were placed in regular employment. The findings indicated that 53% were still employed, and, of the employed, 71% were employed at the same job for more than 12 months. Factors associated with employment were (1) age (16 to 25 years was the modal group—44%), (2) education (59% had some high school or additional education), and (3) never institutionalized (73%).

208. Olshansky, Simon, and Beach, Dorothy. "A Five-Year Follow-Up Study of Physically Disabled Clients." *Rehabilitation Literature*, 36 (August 1975): 251-252, 258.

This is a report of a follow-up study of 229 physically disabled persons who were served in community workshops between January 1969 and December 1973. The study was undertaken in the summer of 1974. 53 or 23.1% of the sample was employed. Factors associated with employment were young age (16 to 19 years), high school graduate, congenitally disabled, and persons who did well at the community workshops.

209. Ortega, Deems F. "Relaxation Exercise with Cerebral Palsied Adults Showing Spasticity." *Journal of Applied Behavior Analysis*, 11, 4 (Winter 1978): 447-451.

This study reports on the testing of relaxation exercises, involving successive tensing and relaxing of major body muscle groups, with four adults with spastic quadriplegia. Subjects showed significant improvement over baseline performance on placing and turning tests following the relaxation technique.

210. Oseroff, Andrew, and Birch, Jack W. "Relationships of Socioeconomic Background and School Performance of Partially Seeing Children." *Exceptional Children*, 38, 2 (October 1971): 158-159.

29 fourth-, fifth-, and sixth-grade students enrolled in special education classes due to partial sight problems were assessed. There were no statistically significant relationships between socioeconomic status and behavioral adjustment mobility or vocational aspiration. Socioeconomic status was significantly related to both age-grade placement and academic achievement. Findings suggest that socioeconomic status is an important factor in determining a student's performance.

211. Parish, Thomas S.; Dyck, Norma; and Koppes, Bruno M. "Stereotypes Concerning Normal and Handicapped Children." *Journal of Psychology*, 102, 1 (May 1979): 63-70.

This is a survey of 65 Kansas school teachers and 89 attendees at a conference of the Association of Children with Learning Disabilities. The subjects were given a list of 50 positive and 50 negative adjectives and asked to select 30 of these to be used in an evaluation of children with given labels. The results were that gifted, normal, and physically handicapped children were rated more positively than mentally retarded, learning disabled, and emotionally disturbed children. The order of this listing corresponds to a rank ordering.

212. Partridge, John W.; Garner, Ann; Thompson, Clare W.; and Cherry, Thomas. "Attitudes of Adolescents Toward Their Diabetes." *American Journal of Diseases of Children*, 124 (August 1972): 226-229.

Teenagers with juvenile diabetes were compared on various dimensions of responsibility to a control group. In most areas, they see themselves similarly. Nondiabetic teenagers feel they took responsibility too early, while those teenagers with diabetes are satisfied with the ages at which they assumed responsibility. Teenagers are ready to begin assuming responsibility for diabetes management at around age 12 and for total management around age 15.

213. Peck, Barbara. "Effects of Childhood Cancer on Long-Term Survivors and Their Families." *British Medical Journal*, 1, 6174 (May 19, 1979): 1327-1329.

A social worker interviewed parents of children treated two years previously for acute lymphatic leukemia and Wilma's tumor. The purpose was to ascertain ways of managing childhood cancer. Findings include: parents expressed the need for more information at time of diagnosis and during subsequent treatment; there is a need for greater continuity of care and involvement of multidisciplinary treatment teams; there is a need for understanding on the part of school teachers that the children have educational needs similar to normal children; there is a need for communication by hospital staff to other family members such as grandparents; parents may need financial help and marital counseling as a result of their child's illness.

214. Peter, John P., and Chinsky, Rosalie R. "Sociological Aspects of Cleft Palate Adults: I. Marriage." *Cleft Palate Journal*, 11, 3 (July 1974): 295-307.

The purpose of this study was to assess the social functioning of adults with cleft lip and/or palate. Survey returns (mailed questionnaires) were received from 196 adult patients, their 190 siblings, and 209 random controls. Results indicated that patients with cleft lip and/or palate were more likely to be single, marry later, or have more childless marriages than the members of the two comparison groups. In relation to age at marriage and number of children, females with cleft lip and palate differed significantly from their controls (married later and had fewer children).

215. Peter, John P., and Chinsky, Rosalie R. "Sociological Aspects of Cleft Palate Adults: II. Education." *Cleft Palate Journal*, 11, 4 (October 1974): 443-449.

This is the second report of a study of the social functioning of adults with cleft lip and/or palate. There were no significant differences in level of education attained for the three groups studied. In relation to educational aspiration, both females with cleft lip and palate and females with cleft palate only, as well as males with cleft lip and palate, had significantly lower aspiration levels than their comparisons. This finding, coupled with the findings regarding marriage for females with cleft lip and palate, leads the authors to conclude that this patient subgroup has lower levels of social acceptance.

216. Peter, John P.; Chinsky, Rosalie R.; and Fisher, Mary J. "Sociological Aspects of Cleft Palate Adults: III. Vocational and Economic Aspects." *Cleft Palate Journal*, 12, 2 (April 1975): 193-199.

This is the third report of a study of the social functioning of adults with cleft lip and/or palate. In relation to social class position and employment stability, there were no significant differences among the three groups studied. However, in regard to gross family income, patients with cleft lip and/or palate scored significantly lower than the two comparison groups.

217. Peter, John P.; Chinsky, Rosalie R.; and Fisher, Mary J. "Sociological Aspects of Cleft Palate Adults: IV. Social Integration." *Cleft Palate Journal*, 12, 3 (July 1975): 304-310.

This is the fourth report of study of the social functioning of adults with cleft lip and/or palate. In regard to geographic mobility, initiating social contacts, and membership in voluntary associations, the patient group scored significantly lower than the two comparison groups.
The findings of the four reports suggest that the goal of rehabilitation is being met in the areas of education and employment. In interpersonal matters, the goal is not being met and particular attention is needed in this area.

218. Peterson, C.; Peterson, J.; and Scriven, G. "Peer Imitation by Nonhandicapped and Handicapped Preschoolers." *Exceptional Children*, 43, 4 (January 1977): 223-224.

Briefly described is a study which tested the hypothesis that nonhandicapped preschoolers constitute more effective models than the handicapped preschoolers for both groups of children. Subjects consisted of 14 handicapped and 15 nonhandicapped children (15 males, 14 females), with each child serving both as subject and model during a task sequence of 10 simple behaviors. Afterward, each child was asked to identify a

photograph of the child he or she preferred to play with. First, second, and third choices were recorded.
Results indicate that both nonhandicapped and handicapped preschool children were more likely to imitate a nonhandicapped peer than a handicapped one. However, this did not appear to be due to the nonhandicapped child's greater ability to perform the behavior to be imitated, since the two types of models did not differ in the accuracy of their presentations.

219. Phillips, Gordon B. "An Exploration of Employer Attitudes Concerning Employment Opportunities for Deaf People." *Journal of Rehabilitation of the Deaf*, 9, 2 (October 1975): 1-9.

This article reports on a survey to identify attitudes which are held by present and potential employers of deaf persons. It identifies attitudes of employers relative to hiring and placement of the deaf, attitudes and opinions of employers regarding the extent to which hearing impairments influence work and productivity, and procedures used by employers to orient deaf individuals to the job.

220. Phillips, Gordon B. "Specific Jobs for Deaf Workers Identified by Employers." *Journal of Rehabilitation of the Deaf*, 9, 2 (October 1975): 10-23.

This article reports on a survey of business and industries, professional and trade organizations, and institutions of higher education for the deaf relative to job opportunities for the deaf. Specific job titles (515) which could be filled by deaf workers are identified. The job titles are coded according to the *Dictionary of Occupational Titles*.

221. Pilowsky, I. "Psychological Aspects of Post-Herpetic Neuralgia: Some Clinical Observations." *British Journal of Medical Psychology*, 50, 4 (December 1977): 283-288.

This study reports on a psychiatric assessment of 10 patients who visited a pain clinic following an attack of shingles. A personality profile characterized by extroversion, obsession, narcissism, and independence is postulated as making the pain of shingles an intolerable imperfection in the person. The study contributes to an understanding of lack of recovery in some cases of shingles where the individual otherwise appears to be in good health.

222. Prino, David. "Personality, Stuttering Severity and Age." *Journal of Speech and Hearing Research*, 15, 1 (March 1972): 148-154.

66 male stutterers between the ages of 8 and 21 years were administered the California Test of Personality and evaluated for stuttering severity during oral reading and spontaneous speech. There were no significant correlations between personality maladjustment and increased age or stuttering severity. Findings support the premise that people who stutter do not seem substantially poorer in personality adjustment than nonstutterers.

223. Quinby, Susan, and Bernstein, Norman R. "Identity Problems and the Adaptation of Nurses to Severely Burned Children." *American Journal of Psychiatry*, 128, 1 (July 1971): 58-63.

This study focused on the adjustment of goals and caring patterns over a one-year period in a new group of nurses in a newly established burn hospital for children. Nurses adjusted expectations from initial expectations of perfection to more mature realistic expectations.

224. Rader, Barbara; Shapiro, Howard L.; and Rodin, Ernest A. "On Placement of Multiply Handicapped Clients into the Open Job Market." *Rehabilitation Literature*, 39, 10 (October 1978): 299-302.

This paper assesses the efforts to place severely disabled epileptic people in competitive employment. The sample consisted of 58 persons with 44 individuals experiencing a workshop phase of rehabilitation, which only 25 persons completed. At a two-year follow-up, only 19 of the 25 persons were still employed. These figures demonstrate that a small number of those eligible completed a training program and are employed two years afterwards. Successful employment is not associated with frequency or type of seizures but the person's intellectual and psychiatric components.

225. Rapier, Jacqueline; Adelson, Ruth; Carey, Richard; and Croke, Katherine. "Changes in Children's Attitudes Toward the Physically Handicapped." *Exceptional Children*, 39, 3 (November 1972): 219-223.

An assessment was made of changes in attitude of 152 elementary school children (third, fourth, and fifth grades) toward orthopedically handicapped children as a result of an integrated school experience. A group administered rating scales based on the semantic differential technique (20 pairs of polar adjectives) was used. Findings indicated that prior to integration, boys perceived handicapped children differently than did girls (wanting more help and being more friendly). After integration, there was no difference between boys and girls in attitude. Older children had a more realistic attitude toward handicapped children than did younger children. Findings showed the importance of providing favorable interactions between handicapped and nonhandicapped children.

226. Reich, Carol M. "The Occupational History of Urban Adults." *Journal of Rehabilitation of the Deaf*, 8, 2 (October 1974): 1-10.

This paper presents data on the occupational status of a group of deaf adults. Data is compared with information on hearing people, many of whom are siblings of the deaf group. Variables examined include: employment rate, job advancement, earnings, job satisfaction, and finding a job. Employment history of the two groups is similar, but present rate of employment of the deaf is lower. Deaf men were as stable, or more stable, in employment patterns than hearing men. The deaf men exhibited little advancement within their jobs, and salaries were lower. The employment rate for deaf women is higher than for hearing women, possibly due to lower economic situation of husbands (often hearing-impaired also). The deaf exhibit a high level of dependency applying for a job or getting a job.

227. Reich, Carol; Hambleton, Donald; and Houldin, Barbara Klein. "The Integration of Hearing Impaired Children in Regular Classrooms." *American Annals of the Deaf*, 122, 6 (December 1977): 534-542.

Levels of integration into normal classroom situations were distinguished. 195 hearing-impaired students in four different levels of integrated class situations were studied. Integration proved beneficial to academic development, but personal and social problems were associated with it. Intelligence and home support were identified as screening factors.

228. Reivich, Ronald S., and Rothrock, Irvin A. "Behavioral Problems of Deaf Children and Adolescents: A Factor-

Analytic Study." *Journal of Speech and Hearing Research*, 15, 1 (March 1972): 93-104.

Using the Quay and Peterson Behavior Problem Checklist, teachers rated 327 students (ages 6 to 20 years) in a state school for the deaf. Factor-analytic techniques indicated that the first three factors extracted, accounting for 70% of the common factor variance, were similar to the conduct, personality, and immaturity dimensions consistently identified in previously studied normal and disturbed populations. Two other factors, labeled isolation and communication problems, were also identified and may represent problem areas specific to deafness.

229. Renne, Charles M., and Creer, Thomas L. "Training Children with Asthma to Use Inhalation Therapy Equipment." *Journal of Applied Behavior Analysis*, 9, 1 (Spring 1976): 1-12.

This study illustrates how children who previously exhibited difficulty in using intermittent positive pressure breathing apparatus were trained through reinforcement techniques. Also discussed are trials with nurses who were being trained to teach children the techniques. The children's use of techniques resulted in reduction of asthma symptoms.

230. Rich, Jordan. "Physical Attractiveness in Teachers' Evaluations." *Journal of Educational Psychology*, 67 (1975): 599-609.

144 teachers rated a pupil after being provided with a photograph of a physically attractive or unattractive child and a vignette describing misbehavior. The attractive child was rated as having a more desirable personality than the unattractive one. Misbehavior was a more serious problem for the unattractive rather than the attractive child.

231. Richardson, Stephen A. "Age and Sex Differences in Values Toward Physical Handicaps." *Journal of Health and Social Behavior*, 11, 3 (September 1970): 207-214.

Children from grades kindergarten to twelve and their parents were exposed to pictures of children with various physical handicaps. Nonhandicapped children were always preferred to handicapped children. Values toward disability gradually changed with age until by the twelfth grade the rating of boys and girls closely resembled those of their parents of the same sex. Their ratings at earlier ages suggest that these values are not acquired from parents. Older females conform more to peer values than older males do. Sex differences include more emphasis on cosmetic effect by females and greater dislike for children with facial disfigurement and the obese; boys showed a lower preference for children with functional handicaps. These findings support traditional stereotypes of female concern with social life and male concern with physical activity.

232. Richardson, Stephen A. "Children's Values and Friendships: A Study of Physical Disability." *Journal of Health and Social Behavior*, 12, 3 (September 1971): 253-258.

This research focuses on children, handicapped and nonhandicapped, and their choice of best friend at summer camp. The research seeks to test the relationship between values and behavior. Children without handicaps, whose individual values toward the handicapped were similar to the group value, chose as best friend someone who was not handicapped; children with individual values that were atypical of the group tended to choose the handicapped as friends. These results emerged after the children had been at camp for two weeks. Children with visible physical handicaps with normative values were more likely to choose as best friend a visibly handicapped child; those with atypical values were more likely to pick a child who was not handicapped.

233. Richardson, Stephen A. "Handicap, Appearance and Stigma." *Social Science and Medicine*, 5, 6 (December 1971): 621-628.

In this research 10- and 11-year-old boys and girls are asked to rank pictures of a child in which everything is held constant except the forms of appearance and handicap. The object of the research is to discover values toward physical appearance and handicap.
From most to least liked, the general rank order of preference was a nonhandicapped white child, a nonhandicapped black child, facial disfigurement, use of a wheelchair, crutches and leg braces, obesity, and amputations. Prostheses increased the rank order of amputees.

It is important to prepare children for the kinds of reactions that handicaps might invoke; it is also important to make adults and others aware of the subtle reactions they may be evidencing toward the handicapped.

234. Richardson, Stephen A., and Emerson, Patricia. "Race and Physical Handicap in Children's Preference for Other Children." *Human Relations*, 23, 1 (February 1970): 31-36.

This research sought to test the relative salience of race and physical handicap in establishing children's preference for other children. The subjects were black girls from the South, 8 to 13 years of age. The authors hypothesized that in an environment of heightened racial awareness, the cues of physical disability would not mask the effects of color. Research in the North had previously indicated otherwise. Race was a more salient factor for the new test group, but handicap was also salient. The black girls showed some self-devaluation and preference for white over black. They conformed to dominant group values in the same way that handicapped children showed preference for nonhandicapped in earlier research.

235. Richardson, Stephen A., and Friedman, Matthew J. "Social Factors Related to Children's Accuracy in Learning Peer Group Values Towards Handicaps." *Human Relations*, 26, 1 (February 1973): 77-87.

The purpose of this study is to explore the process by which children learn values. Emphasis is on variables related to the acquisition of normative values. Children in summer camps and school settings were asked to react to pictures of children with varied handicaps. Their reactions are related to sociometric choice. The researchers found that children who receive a larger number of friendship choices from their peers express a normative value toward disability, while children who receive few friendship choices express an atypical value toward disability. Peer group was found to be influential in normative learning toward handicap among younger boys, but among older boys only when a clear relationship exists between sociometric status and a normative value. Thus, for boys, structure of peer group becomes more important in determining values with age. For girls, peers exerted no detectable influence as a source of learning values.

The Studies

The research did not present detailed evidence on parental influence in the learning of values toward the handicapped.

236. Richardson, Stephen A.; Ronald, Linda; and Klech, Robert E. "The Social Status of Handicapped and Nonhandicapped Boys in a Camp Setting." *Journal of Special Education*, 8 (1974): 143-152.

The subjects were 193 boys attending the Fresh Air Fund summer camps during the summer of 1971. In relation to evaluation as persons and preferences as friends, visibly handicapped were least preferred, non-visibly handicapped were in an intermediate position and the nonhandicapped boys were the most preferred. Further analysis indicated that the visibly handicapped boys were also the least skilled in social relationships, which may account for their being least preferred. The authors state that further study is needed to clarify the relationship between interpersonal skill, intrapersonal evaluation, and physical appearance.

237. Richman, Lynn C. "Behavior and Achievement of Cleft Palate Children." *Cleft Palate Journal*, 13, (January 1976): 4-10.

The purpose of this study was to assess the relationship between the cleft palate condition and the child's school behavior and achievement. The patient group consisted of 44 children between the ages of 9 and 14 years who were matched on age, sex, and socioeconomic status with 44 noncleft children. The Behavior Problem Checklist developed by Quay and Peterson was used as the basis for the Teachers' Rating as was the Iowa Test of Basic Skills. Findings were as follows:
  (1) There were no cleft type differences noted.
  (2) Children with cleft lip and/or palate were rated by teachers as displaying significantly greater inhibition of impulse.
  (3) The patient group also scored significantly lower on overall achievement.

238. Richman, Lynn C. "The Effect of Facial Disfigurement on Teachers' Perceptions of Ability in Cleft Palate Children." *Cleft Palate Journal*, 15, 2 (April 1978): 155-160.

This investigation assessed the relationship between facial appearance in children with cleft lip and/or palate and the accuracy of teachers' ratings of intellectual ability. The 87 children with cleft lip and/or palate, between the ages of 9 to 14 years, were divided into two groups on the basis of independent ratings of facial appearance. The two groups did not differ on intellectual behavior, or achievement data. All the children were enrolled in regular classrooms. The results of the classroom teachers' estimates of intellectual functioning indicated that they rated children with more noticeable facial disfigurement less accurately than children with relatively normal facial appearance. This finding suggests that the teachers are operating on cultural stereotypes, relating physical unattractiveness to decreased intellectual ability.

239. Richman, Lynn C. "Parents and Teachers: Differing Views of Behavior of Cleft Palate Children." *Cleft Palate Journal*, 15, 4 (October 1978): 360-364.

This study compared mothers', fathers', and teachers' perceptions of behavior of 136 children with cleft lip and/or palate between the ages of 7 and 12 years. The comparisons were made on the behavioral dimensions of inhibitions and acting out as measured by the Quay and Peterson Behavior Checklist. The teachers rated the children as significantly more inhibited in the classroom than parents observed at home. Fathers and mothers concur in their ratings and differ from teachers in that they do not view their children as excessively inhibited.

240. Richman, Lynn C., and Harper, Dennis C. "Self-Identified Personality Patterns of Children with Facial or Orthopedic Disfigurement." *Cleft Palate Journal*, 16 (1979): 257-261.

This study compared personality characteristics of children with cleft lip and palate to a group of children with orthopedic disability. 45 children from each group were matched for sex, age, and intelligence. Both groups were administered the Missouri Children's Picture Test Series. The results indicated that males with cleft lip and palate are significantly higher on maturity and inhibition while orthopedically disabled males are higher on aggression, activity level, and somatization. Cleft lip and palate females are significantly higher on maturity and inhibition while orthopedically disabled females are higher on masculinity. The authors conclude that the results indicate differential personality adaptations in these two types of observable physical impairments.

241. Roberts, Joan I. "Dual Discrimination: The Interaction Between Sex Roles and Disabilities." *American Archives of Rehabilitation Therapy*, 25, 2 (Summer 1977): 1-7.

This article explores the societal context in which disabilities occur, particularly the cultural roles of males and females. Bemoaning the lack of statistical analyses relating to sex roles and disabilities in documents reporting on social insurance, welfare services, and vocational rehabilitation, the author reviews theories and processes described in major texts used to train professionals in this area. Research studies on the relationship between disability and attitudes, emotional factors, and sensory-perceptual processes in men and women are discussed. Little concern for the variations or similarities in male and female deviations form the psychological or physical norms, as found in the literature, is noted.

242. Rosenberg, J. "The Relationship of Types of Post-High School Education to Occupation and Economic Independence of Physically Handicapped Adults." *Rehabilitation Literature*, 38, 2 (February 1978): 45-49.

The sample for this study were 79 orthopedically handicapped students of a public school. The findings were as follows:
   (1) The alumnus with the best chance for full economic functioning is the moderately handicapped graduate with vocational training or a college education leading to a position in areas of the occupational structure where opportunities are protected by law.
   (2) In view of the fact that the ability and the opportunity to perform economic roles and to maintain financial self-sufficiency are at the core of an adult identity, it is important that further research be done with larger handicapped populations in order to clarify the relationship of educational and career choices to employment and earnings.

243. Rosenbloom, Alfred A. "Prognostic Factors in the Visual Rehabilitation of Aging Patients." *New Outlook for the Blind*, 68, 3 (March 1974): 124-127.

The subjects for this study were 150 patients between the ages of 60 and 89 years. The focus was on factors related to successful visual rehabilitation as measured by successful use of low vision aids. 84% of the subjects were successful. Factors related to success were: ocular pathology, degree of residual vision, type of aid prescribed, psychological adjustment to life and to visual problems. Training in the use of vision aids was identified as an important factor in successful adaptation to the aid.

244. Rutzen, Robert S. "The Social Importance of Orthodontic Rehabilitation: Report of a Five Year Follow-Up Study." *Journal of Health and Social Behavior*, 14, 3 (September 1973): 233-240.

The purpose of this research is to see if persons who receive orthodontic treatment experience less social discrimination than those persons with untreated malocclusions. 252 treated persons were interviewed five years after treatment. They were compared on a number of social and psychological variables to 67 persons with untreated malocclusions.

The treated persons scored slightly higher on occupational rank, but not in social class or educational achievement. The treated persons were slightly more likely to be engaged or married, but did not differ from the untreated in dating patterns. More often than the untreated, the treated persons assessed themselves as having improved physical appearance, but did not have higher self-esteem. The untreated had higher anxiety, but this was not statistically significant. The two groups did not differ on extroversion or neuroticism.

Malocclusion may not be a strong reason for social discrimination.

245. Sadlick, Marie, and Penta, Frank B. "Changing Nurse Attitudes Toward Quadriplegics Through Use of Television." *Rehabilitation Literature*, 36, 9 (September 1975): 274-278, 288.

The attitudes of 44 senior nursing students in a medical surgical nursing course emphasizing rehabilitation were studied before and after the presentation of a 17-minute videotape of a successfully rehabilitated quadriplegic. The attitudes of the student nurses were significantly altered in a positive direction. The changes persisted throughout the ten-week course. However, while still significant, the positive attitude had diminished. The authors interpret this to support the idea that the videotape, rather than the rehabilitation course, was more effective in altering the attitudes of the student in a positive direction.

246. Salk, Lee; Hilgartner, Margaret; and Granich, Bell. "The Psycho-Social Impact of Hemophilia on the Patient and His Family." *Social Science and Medicine*, 6, 4 (August 1972): 491-505.

This is exploratory research conducted at the New York Hospital Hemophilia Clinic. It is a study of 26 families with 32 hemophiliacs who had multiple types of hemophilia. The parents believed the disease had a negative influence on the family relationships, but the patients did not think so. Social mobility was also affected because of the need to be near a major medical center.

The research discusses both the patients' and the parents' perception of restrictions resulting from the illness. With certain positive adjustments, these families seem to have a family life similar to the general population. Recommendations are made to assist the adjustment of patients and families to the illness.

247. Samerotte, George C., and Harris, Mary B. "Some Factors Influencing Helping: The Effects of a Handicap, Responsiblity, and Requesting Help." *Journal of Social Psychology*, 98, 1 (February 1976): 39-45.

In an experiment, the dropping of envelopes while walking in a shopping center, confederates played various handicapped roles. More help was rendered to role players with a bandage around the forearm than to others with an eye patch or facial scar, and with a bandage than with a scar or no handicap. When subjects were led to feel responsible for the role player's accident, more help was offered. Males offered more help than females. This study combines the theory that handicap increases sympathy with the theory that disfigurement reduces attractiveness.

248. Sands, H., and Zalkind, S.S. "Effects of an Educational Campaign to Change Employer Attitudes Toward Hiring Epileptics." *Epilepsia*, 13 (1972): 87-96.

Pre- and post-attitude data were obtained from 69 respondents in the experimental city and 80 in the control city. An intensive educational campaign, including the movie, "The Dark Wave," was used in the experimental city. The Community Health Survey was administered to assess attitudes. No significant differences were found in the comparison of the data for the two groups. Despite respondents positive working experiences with epileptics, they did not feel that they could hire more epileptics. Only 2% of the rehabilitated patients hired are epileptics. Employer resistance was identified as the largest factor responsible for unemployment of persons with epilepsy.

249. Santopietro, Mary-Charles S. "Meeting the Emotional Needs of Hemodialysis Patients and Their Spouses." *American Journal of Nursing*, 75, 4 (April 1975): 629-632.

This article reports interview material derived from 12 male dialysis patients and their wives. The focus is on how nurses can help the couples cope. Patient needs are identified. They include the need for identity, the need to grieve, need for safety and control of the environment, need for communication, need for love, and the need to establish one's optimum level of wellness.

250. Sanua, Victor D. "A Cross Cultural Study of Cerebral Palsy." *Social Science and Medicine*, 4, 4 (August 1979): 461-512.

This study is based on research with 205 individuals with cerebral palsy from vocational and rehabilitation facilities in eight different countries. The purpose was to see if cultural values influence attitudes of the physically handicapped and nonhandicapped toward the disabled. The countries were classified as near or below the Mediterranean. Various objective and projective psychological tests were administered, with the main test being the Attitude Toward Disabled Persons Scale. In general, cultural factors appeared to be important variables in determining individual attitudes and plans. The more supportive cultural definitions were associated with more positive psychological states of individual cerebral palsy victims.

251. Sarfaty, Linda, and Katz, Shlomo. "The Self-Concept and Adjustment Patterns of Hearing-Impaired Pupils in Different School Settings." *American Annals of the Deaf*, 123, 4 (June 1978): 438-441.

Using ninth-grade students in Israel, this study tests whether hearing-impaired children in integrative school settings have different self-concepts and different adjustment patterns than hearing-impaired pupils in a special school setting. The pupils in the integrative settings did have higher self-concepts, but the adjustment profiles did not differ.

252. Sayed, Alae-Eldin. "A Survey of Children's Social Attitudes Toward Disability." *American Archives of Rehabilitation Therapy*, 24, 1 (Spring 1976): 15-16.

    This is a survey of 23 nonhandicapped children who attended a two-week summer camp while another camp for handicapped children was in session. The objective was to ascertain nondisabled children's attitudes toward disability. Findings are presented in the context of how in the face of "mainstreaming," normal children might react to handicapped and disabled children in the classroom. Generally, attitudes were favorable. No statistically significant differences were found between a pre- and post-test, with most changes in opinions toward a favorable of "not sure" response.

253. Sayed, Alae-Eldin. "Social Attitudes Toward the Handicapped: A Survey of Sophomore Students at Northeastern University." *American Archives of Rehabilitation Therapy*, 24, 1 (Spring 1976): 17.

    Students at Northeastern University were sampled concerning their attitudes about disabled persons. Tabulated responses are reported on dating, considering marriage, willingness to marry a person with one of the following disabilities: blind, hard of hearing, amputee, person using crutches, facial or body disfigurement, cerebral palsy, epilepsy.

254. Sayed, Alae-Eldin. "Social Attitudes of University Students Toward the Disabled: Contributory Factors." *American Archives of Rehabilitation Therapy*, 26, 1-2 (Spring-Summer 1978): 26-28.

    This survey of sophomores at Northeastern University investigates attitudes of normal students toward the social integration of disabled students. Findings include: previous contact with handicapped leads to more favorable attitude; the more often the contact, the better the attitude and vise versa; females have more positive attitudes than males; major in a helping or people-oriented field of study correlates with higher rate of tolerance for disabled; students showed higher commitment to less intensive, less permanent relationships such as dating rather than marriage; individuals with mild disabilities had a better chance of social acceptance than those with more severe disability; visible disabilities are associated with lower social acceptance.

255. Schindele, Rudolf. "The Social Adjustment of Visually Handicapped Children in Different Educational Settings." *American Foundation for the Blind Research Bulletin*, 28 (October 1974): 125-142.

This study compares the self-concept social adjustment scores of three groups: visually handicapped students integrated in resource or itinerant programs in regular schools, visually handicapped children from residential schools, and sighted control subjects. There was no significant difference between visually handicapped and sighted students in social adjustment. There was no significant difference between the two groups of visually handicapped students. Other findings include the fact that intelligence and social adjustment correlate significantly for the integrated visually handicapped sample, but not for the other samples. A significant inverse correlation exists between socioeconomic status and social adjustment for visually handicapped students in residential schools, but not in the other two samples.

256. Schmale, A.H., and Iker, H. "Hopelessness as a Predictor of Cervical Cancer." *Social Science and Medicine*, 5, 2 (April 1971): 95-100.

The subjects for this research were 17 women considered "biologically predisposed" to cervical cancer. Subjects were classified as having a "hopelessness prone personality" versus those subjects not considered to be "hopeless prone."
Those classified as "hopeless prone" through interview data were found to have higher rates of cancer based on pathological reports of bone biopsies than those not classified as "hopeless prone." The researchers raise the possibility that the effect of hopelessness or personality predisposition of hopelessness may act as a facilitating or promoter agent for cervical carcinoma in women who have cervical dysplasia.

257. Schofield, Larry, and Kunce, Joseph. "Client Disability and Counselor Behavior." *Rehabilitation Counseling Bulletin*, 14, 3 (March 1971): 158-165.

6 vocational rehabilitation counselors were studied to assess the nature of their perceptions and treatment of handicapped clients. A seven-point scale was used to assess the counselor's judgments in relation to clients' workshop performance, employability dropout rate and work adjustment. Physically disabled clients were viewed as more employable than were mentally retarded or emotionally disturbed clients. These attitudes will affect a client's future, regardless of his current level of social functioning. Supervision and in-service training is needed concerning the harm of negative attitude.

258. Schwab, Lois O. "Rehabilitation of Physically Disabled Women in a Family-Oriented Program." *Rehabilitation Literature*, 36, 2 (February 1975): 34-43, 47.

The sample consisted of 22 homemakers and their families in an experimental group and the same number in a comparison group. Families were matched on the basis of operational functioning of the disabled mother, socioeconomic class, and family responsibilities. The findings did not show any significant differences between the two types of rehabilitation programs.

259. Schweckendiek, Wolfram, and Danzer, Claus. "Psychological Studies in Patients with Clefts." *Cleft Palate Journal*, 7, 2 (April 1970): 533-539.

200 patients with cleft lip and/or palate ranging in age from 7 to 14 years were studied in regard to behavior at home and in school. 75% of the children were functioning at their appropriate age level on the various measures (questionnaires completed by parents and teachers). These measures included school achievement, IQ testing, and speech status.

260. Segal, J.J.; Chagoya, L.; Villenewve, C.; and Mayerovitch, J. "Later Psychosocial Sequelae of Early Childhood Illness." *American Journal of Psychiatry*, 130, 7 (July 1973): 786-789.

This is a follow-up of 12 families in which only one child had had severe croup before age five. Children rated parents' attitudes toward them and parents rated their behavior toward the child and one sibling. The "vulnerable child" syndrome is described as a result of disturbances in the parent-child relationship following early childhood illness. Relations of independence-dependence are reported. Factors reported elsewhere as being related to successful rehabilitation emerge as part of the syndrome.

261. Seidel, U.P.; Chadwick, O.F.D.; and Rutter, M. "Psychological Disorders in Crippled Children. A Comparative Study of Children with and without Brain Damage." *Developmental Medicine and Child Neurology*, 17, 5 (October 1975): 563-573.

   A detailed, standardized study was made of all handicapped children who were between 5 and 15 years of age, had normal intelligence, and were included on the local authority lists of handicapped children in three London boroughs. Findings indicate that psychiatric disorder is twice as common among handicapped children when their physical condition involves disease or damage of the brain. Because groups were well matched in terms of physical incapacity and social background, it was concluded that brain damage was responsible for the children's increased vulnerability to emotional problems. Brain damage was also associated with a marked increase in reading difficulties and with a lowering of intelligence within the normal range. Psychiatric disorder was found to be related, not only to cerebral injury but also to various types of family disturbances. It is concluded that emotional and behavioral disturbance steemed from a combination of increased biological vulnerability and psychosocial hazards.

262. Serunian, Sally A., and Broman, Sarah H. "Relationship of Apgar Scores and Bayley Mental and Motor Scores." *Child Development*, 46, 3 (September 1975): 696-700.

   The higher the Apgar score, the healthier is the infant at birth. 350 subjects were followed from birth to eight months of age when they were tested on the Bayley Scales. Correlation indicated significant relationships between the Apgar scores and the Bayley scores for mental and motor behavior. These correlations were independent of the child's birth weight.

263. Shapiro, Sam; Weinblatt, Eve; Frank, Charles W.; and Sager, Robert V. "Social Factors in the Prognosis of Men Following First Myocardial Infarction." *Milbank Memorial Fund Quarterly*, 48, 1 (January 1970): 37-50.

The data is from the Health Insurance Plan of Greater New York study of the incidence and prognosis of coronary heart disease among a population of 110,000 men and women, ages 25 to 64 years, for the period 1961 to 1965. Observations reported are for one month, six months, and four years following myocardial infarction. Emphasis is on social factors. Color and religion show different directional relations for incidence and prognosis: nonwhite and non-Jewish men have relatively high death rates immediately after the myocardial infarction; cardiac mortality persists at a higher rate for these groups than for others. Cardiac death rates among the blue collar men is 1.6 times the rate among white collar men. Education and religion do not explain the higher rate among blue collar men. Myocardial infarction is followed by greater life style changes in the socioeconomic group with the poorest prognosis.

264. Shealy, Allen E. "Comparison of Two Non-Intellective Scales of Intelligence and Their Relationship to Intellectual Change Following Surgery." *Psychological Reports*, 42 (1978): 51-56.

The WAIS, Bender-Gestalt test, and the MMPI were administered to 102 cardiac patients two days prior to cardiac surgery and again six days postoperatively. The findings indicate no significant decrease in the WAIS from pre- to post-surgery. Furthermore, preoperative intellectual efficiency as measured by the MMPI was not predictive of changes in intellectual and perceptual motor ability.

265. Shekelle, R.B.; Ostfeld, A.M.; Lebovits, B.Z.; and Oglesby, P. "Personality Traits and Coronary Heart Disease: A Re-Examination of Ibrahim's Hypothesis Using Longitudinal Data." *Journal of Chronic Diseases*, 23 (1970): 33-38.

80 patients with coronary heart diseases were studied longitudinally. No personality trait differences were noted in this sample of industrial employees. Also there were no significant differences in psychological patterns among groups characterized by low, moderately high, and high risk of coronary heart disease.

266. Shipley, Robert H.; O'Donnell, John M.; and Boder, Karl F. "Personality Characteristics of Women Seeking Breast Augmentation." *Plastic and Reconstructive Surgery*, 60 (1977): 369-376.

Three groups of 28 subjects each participated in the study: augmentation, small breasts, and average size breasts. The three groups were compared on California Psychological Inventory, Ziller Social Self-Esteem Test, Attitude Toward Women Scale, and Body Attitude Scale. The three groups were similar except that those seeking augmentation negatively evaluated their breasts and placed greater emphasis on dress and physical attractiveness.

267. Shontz, Franklin C. "Forces Influencing the Decision to Seek Medical Care." *Rehabilitation Psychology*, 21, 3 (Fall 1974): 86-94.

A group of college students was given test forms that stated they were seeking medical care from one of three sources: family physician, an unknown private physician, or the university clinic. Another group in the community was given the same forms, but excluding the university clinic as a possible source of help. The subjects all indicated how strongly any of 17 factors would influence their decision to seek care. The strongest force for seeking help was the desire to return to health and to have symptom relief. Strongest resistance in seeking care centered on dislike or distrust of the physician. The article highlights how doctor-patient relationships enter into patient decisions about health care. This is important given the need for a continuing relationship for rehabilitation.

268. Sieka, Frank L. "Facial Disfigurement and Sex-Role Esteem." *Rehabilitation Counseling Bulletin*, 18, 2 (December 1974): 90-98.

40 adult patients with facial disfigurement (cancer and accidents) were compared to 50 adults with no facial disfigurement. Both groups completed the Acceptance Toward Disability Scale, the Semantic Differential to assess sex role concept, and the Demographic Data Inventory. The results indicated that the patient group felt themselves to be less positive as males or females compared to the control group. The younger the patient and the more severe the facial disfigurement (self-perceived) were associated with negative ratings of sex-role concept. Acceptance of disability was positively correlated with positive sex role assessment.

269. Silverman, Ellen Marie, and Zimmer, Catherine H. "Women Who Stutter: Personality and Speech Character-

istics." *Journal of Speech and Hearing Research*, 22 (1979): 553-564.

10 adult female stutterers, 10 adult male stutterers, and 10 adult female nonstutterers were administered the California Test of Personality and Semantic Differential Forms, designed to assess self-concept. The female stutterers evidenced a significantly higher level of self-esteem than the male stutterers. Moreover, unlike the male stutterers, the female stutterers did not consider themselves handicapped. These findings suggest that the personality characteristics of stutterers may differ by gender.

270. Simonds, John F., and Heimburger, Richard E. "Psychiatric Evaluation of Youth with Cleft Lip-Palate Matched with a Control Group." *Cleft Palate Journal*, 15, 3 (July 1978): 193-201.

40 randomly selected patients with cleft lip and/or palate between the ages of 6 and 18 years were matched for age, sex, and socioeconomic status with 40 patients in a control group from a family practice clinic. Both groups were interviewed by a child psychiatrist and the mothers completed a behavior checklist. There were no significant differences in the number of subjects from both groups having psychiatric diagnoses or conflicts. Mothers' ratings indicated that the patient group had significantly more subjects with excessive dependency problems. Cleft type differences occurred with male cleft palate only, and female cleft lip and palate had more psychiatric problems compared to female cleft palate only and male cleft lip and palate.

271. Smith, Clyde R. "The Relationship Between Self-Concept and Success in the Freshman Year of College." *New Outlook for the Blind*, 66, 3 (March 1972): 84-89.

This study investigates the relationship between self-concept and success in the freshman year of college. Two groups of blind freshman college students, those who persisted and those who did not, were compared on self-concept as measured by the Tennessee Self Concept Scale. This scale is a semantic differential that is supposed to be significant for blind students. The results indicate that the scale may be useful to differentiate between persisting and nonpersisting students and in identification of attitudes that contribute to blind students chances for successful completion of the freshman year at college.

272. Smits, Stanley; Conire, Tali; and Edwards, Larry. "Definitions of Disability as Determinants of Scores on the Attitude Toward Disabled Persons Scale." *Rehabilitation Counseling Bulletin*, 14, 4 (June 1971): 227-235.

Age and educational level were varied to assess their association with Attitude Toward Disabled Persons Scale. 216 college students, 95% under 21 years of age, were compared with teachers who were over 21. Teachers were found to have a broader definition of disabled than the students. Female teachers had a more favorable attitude than male teachers. Students with contact with physically disabled persons had more favorable attitudes.

273. Sobel, Harry J., and Worden, J. William. "The MMPI as a Predictor of Psychosocial Adaptation to Cancer." *Journal of Consulting and Clinical Psychology*, 47, 4 (August 1979): 716-724.

In this study the Minnesota Multiphasic Personality Inventory (MMPI) was examined as a longitudinal predictor of psychosocial adaptation to cancer. Results indicated that on the basis of initial screening with the MMPI, 75% of all patients newly diagnosed with cancer could have been correctly classified into a high-distressed versus a low-distressed cancer patient group.

274. Starr, Philip. "Hospitalization Effects upon Behavior of Pre-Schoolers with Cleft Lip and/or Palate: A Pilot Study." *Cleft Palate Journal*, 15, 2 (April 1978): 182-185.

The hypothesis that the number of hospitalizations adversely affects the behavior of 3- to 5-year-old preschool children with cleft lip and/or palate was investigated in a pilot study. The study consisted of 22 patients of the Lancaster Cleft Palate Clinic who were hospitalized three or more times. The comparison group was 23 children without a cleft condition who had not been hospitalized at the time of data collection. Both groups were matched in age, sex, and family socioeconomic status. The mothers completed the Missouri Children's Behavior Checklist for their children. There were no statistically significant differences between the two groups on the six behavioral dimensions of the Missouri Checklist.

275. Starr, Philip. "Self-Esteem and Behavioral Functioning of Teen-Agers with Oral-Facial Clefts." *Rehabilitation Literature*, 39, 8 (August 1978): 233-235.

This paper reports the results of a study of 72 teenagers who were patients at the H.K. Cooper Clinic and who were compared with 48 teenagers without a cleft condition. The two groups were matched for age, sex, and family socioeconomic status. The findings were as follows:
   (1) The only statistically significant difference between the two groups was that the teenagers with oral-facial clefts were less physically aggressive the controls.
   (2) Attitude toward clefting is an important variable in determining a person's behavior, supporting the premise that a person's acceptance of the disability is likely to be associated with better adjustment.

276. Starr, Philip, and Heiserman, Kitty. "Acceptance of Disability by Teen-Agers with Oral-Facial Clefts." *Rehabilitation Counseling Bulletin*, 20, 3 (March 1977): 198-201.

The purpose of this study was to assess the degree of acceptance of disability in the sample of 72 teenage patients of the Lancaster Cleft Palate Clinic. The Acceptance of Disability Scale was modified by use of the word clefting in place of disability. Findings were as follows:
   (1) There was no difference in attitude toward disability by cleft type.
   (2) The extremely favorable attitude towards clefting group scored higher on self-esteem and behavior scores as measured by the Missouri Children's Behavior Checklist compared to the extremely unfavorable group of patients.
Findings can be interpreted to support the premise that denial is an unsatisfactory coping technique.

277. Starr, Philip; Chinsky, Rosalie; Canter, Harry; and Meier, Joseph. "Mental, Motor and Social Behavior of Infants with Cleft Lip and/or Palate." *Cleft Palate Journal*, 14, 2 (April 1977): 140-147.

This is a report of analyses of cross-sectional and longitudinal samples of the mental, motor, and social behavior of children with cleft lip and/or palate as measured by the Bayley Scales for Infant Development. 75 patients of the Lancaster Cleft Palate Clinic were the subjects for the sample. The longitudinal sample consisted of 28 of these patients for whom there were complete data at 6, 12, 18, and 24 months. The results indicated no significant differences in mental and motor functioning. In both analyses, the social behavior of patients with cleft lip and/or palate was more passive than the normative sample.

278. Stehbens, James A., and MacQueen, John C. "The Psychological Adjustment of Rheumatic Fever Patients with and without Chorea: Comparisons Ten Years Later." *Clinical Pediatrics*, 11 (November 1972): 638-640.

65 adult patients with rheumatic fever with chorea were assessed on the Minnesota Multiphasic Personality Inventory (MMPI). They were matched for sex and age with 65 patients who had rheumatic fever but did not have chorea. There were no significant differences between the two groups as measured by the MMPI. These findings do not support the notion that the former group will more likely have personality maladjustment problems in adulthood.

279. Storer, R.D.K. "The Vocational Boundaries of Deaf and Partially-Hearing Adolescents and Young Adults in the West Midlands." *British Association of Teachers of the Deaf*, 1, 4 (July 1977): 134-136.

This is a report on a survey of 49 deaf and hearing-impaired adolescents from the British West Midlands during the period 1969 to 1974. The survey seeks to measure the social and vocational adjustment of the subjects. Occupational distributions are reported according to sex of respondent. Conclusions reached include: the deaf and hearing impaired are largely underemployed and restricted to a narrow range of occupations; they and significant others are unaware of the employment opportunities available.

280. Strauss, Gordon D.; Pedersen, Susan; and Dudovitz, Dorothy. "Psychosocial Support for Adults with Cystic Fibrosis." *American Journal of Diseases of Children*, 133, 3 (March 1979): 301-305.

This article describes a group of adults with cystic fibrosis (CF), a disease about which we have limited knowledge for adult victims. Issues raised by patients include doubts about the competence of nonpediatricians to treat CF; resentment toward normal adults, including health professionals; desire to gain more control over the management of their own life. The article stresses the use of groups for treating CF adults.

281. Streltzer, Jon; Finkelstein, Frederic; Feigenbaum, Helen; Kitsen, Jenny; and Cohn, George L. "The Spouse's Role in Home Hemodialysis." *Archives of General Psychiatry*, 33 (January 1976): 55-58.

    This article is a series of case illustrations on the type of responses spouses have made to home dialysis. Success in home dialysis is "at risk" when the spouse is naturally dependent on the patient-partner. Spouses often require special support.

282. Styczynski, Lyn E.; and Langlois, Judith H. "The Effects of Familiarity on Behavioral Stereotypes Associated with Physical Attractiveness in Young Children." *Child Development*, 58, 3 (September 1977): 1137-1141.

    The subjects were 44 children, 24 males and 20 females, who ranged in age from 3 to 7 years. Acquainted and unacquainted raters agreed on judgments of physical attractiveness. For unacquainted raters, the results indicated that they viewed unattractive children as more likely to behave in an antisocial manner than attractive children. For acquainted raters, the ratings were contradictory. These findings suggest that the former ratings were based on stereotypes, while the latter ratings were based on a complex interaction of factors.

283. Sussman, Marvin B.; Haug, Marie R.; Hagan, Frank E.; Kitson, Gary C.; and Williams, Gwendolyn K. "Rehabilitation Counseling in Transition: Some Findings." *Journal of Rehabilitation*, 41, 3 (May-June 1975): 27-33, 40.

    This reports on a 1965 study of 324 graduates of federally funded rehabilitation training schools. These students were found to be different from other graduate students in the United States. They were more likely to be disabled, second careerists, from working and lower class backgrounds, and of minority social groups. One year after graduation, one-third of the graduates were not working in rehabilitation counseling.

A study conducted in 1972 with 739 graduates revealed that this group, as contrasted to the 1965 group, had a smaller proportion of minorities, second careerists, disabled, and higher proportion of counselors under the age of 30. The authors argue that these differences are indicative of growing professionalization of the role of rehabilitation counselor.

284. Taylor, George P., Jr., and Persons, Roy W. "Behavior Modification Techniques in a Physical Medicine and Rehabilitation Center." *Journal of Psychology*, 74, 1 (January 1970): 117-124.

This is a research report on three case studies in which behavior modification techniques were employed in rehabilitation. Two studies involve quadriplegics and the third a patient with multiple sclerosis. The aim is to show that behavior modification techniques are useful in physical rehabilitation, that they can readily be taught to staff, and that they can be used with various disabilities.

285. Thomas, Elizabeth C., and Yamamoto, Kaoru. "School-Related Perceptions in Handicapped Children." *Journal of Psychology*, 7, 1 (January 1971): 101-117.

500 middle and high school students were administered a semantic differential test. The students were grouped according to four types of handicap: mentally retarded, disturbed, blind, and deaf. Attitudes toward people (parents, teachers, classmates, and self) and attitudes toward curriculum (social studies, language, science, and mathematics) were studied.

Most significant were effects of handicap on all concepts. The findings indicate that there is no monolithic handicapped group and that differential preparation is needed for individuals aspiring to teach each group.

In the people ratings, the general overall ordered ratings were parents, teachers, self, and classmates. However, teachers received low ratings on security. This raises questions relative to the mental hygiene environment of the classroom. Other findings included a decrease in self-esteem as age increased and a low rating of social studies curriculum by the retarded, the blind, and the deaf.

286. Thomas, K.R.; Davis, R.M.; and Hochman, M.E. "Correlates of Disability Acceptance in Amputees." *Rehabilitation Bulletin*, 19, 3 (March 1976): 505-511.

This study investigated the relationships between selected sociopsychological characteristics of the physically disabled and their acceptance of disability. Subjects were 51 of 87 amputees who were receiving or had received services from a state vocational rehabilitation agency as of March 1973. 27 client characteristics were treated as independent variables. The dependent variable, acceptance of disability, was operationally defined as the client's score on Linkowski's (1971) Acceptance of Disability Scale. Statistical analysis indicated significance on only 3 of 27 variables, while trends toward significance were observed on 5 others. In addition, findings suggest that the socioeconomic aspects of an occupation (the social status and salary of a person's job) may be less critical to acceptance than whether a change in occupation or vocational plans is necessitated by onset of disability.

287. Tolor, Alexander; Tolor, Belle; and Blumin, Shirley S. "Self-Concept and Locus of Control in Primary-Grade Children Identified as Requiring Special Educational Programing." *Psychological Reports*, 40 (1977): 43-49.

A group of 28 children from kindergarten through grade 4, presenting a variety of learning-related problems, were compared with a matched group of 28 control children on the Revised Self-Appraisal Inventory, and the Preschool and Primary Internal-External Control Scale. Findings indicated that the problem children exhibited less positive self-concepts relative to controls, but there was no difference between the two groups of children in relation to locus of control. The authors concluded that the Self-Appraisal Inventory is a useful measure that might be helpful in evaluating special education programs.

288. Touliatos, John, and Lindholm, Byron W. "Influence of Parental Expectancies and Responsiveness of Achievement Motivation of Minimally Brain-Impaired and Normal Children." *Psychological Reports*, 35, 1, Part 2 (August 1974): 395-400.

16 families with minimally brain injured (MBI) children and 16 families with normal children were matched on a number of characteristics. Findings were as follows:
   (1) Mothers of MBI children had lower expectancies concerning achievement than did mothers of normal children. There was no difference among fathers.

(2) MBI children were lower in need for achievement than the normal children.

289. Tringo, John L. "The Hierarchy of Preference Toward Disability Groups." *Journal of Special Education*, 4, 3 (Summer-Fall 1970): 295-305.

A study to investigate different attitudes toward specific disability groups was undertaken by the author. He hypothesized that: (1) a hierarchy of preference exists with respect to disability groups; (2) demographic variables of the nondisabled affect the extent of social distance expressed toward specific disability groups but do not affect the relative position of disability groups in the hierarchy; (3) females express less social distance (more acceptance) toward disability groups than do males; (4) an increase in education results in an increase in acceptance of disability groups. The Disability Social Distance Scale (DSDS) was developed, based on the original Social Distance Scale of Bogardus. Punishment items ("Would put to death") were added to the 21 items selected to represent various stages of social distance in an attempt to tap the more extreme range of social distance not included in the original scale.

The first three hypotheses were confirmed. The fourth hypothesis could be confirmed only for the confounded variables of age and education. The composition of the hierarchy of preference followed the general order suggested in previous studies, that is, physically disabled first, sensorily disabled second, and brain injured third. Alcoholism and mental illness were found to be less preferred than physical disabilities. A physical disability (tuberculosis) ranked low. The author attributed it to contagious connotation. Dwarf and hunchback rated low. The influence of an aesthetic factor was suggested. Three major causes of death and disability in the U.S., heart disease, stroke, and cancer, were rated relatively high in preference.

290. Tropauer, Alan; Franz, Martha Neal; and Dilgard, Victor W. "Psychological Aspects of the Care of Children with Cystic Fibrosis." *American Journal of Diseases of Children*, 119, 5 (May 1970): 424-432.

Interviews and psychological tests were used with a group of children with cystic fibrosis and their mothers. Physical and social restrictions, the medical regimen, concerns about illness and death, and uncertainty as to future were identified as factors leading to anxiety and depression in children and mothers. It is important to identify sources of depression because emotional conflicts in either mother or child can lead to maladaptive behavior or resistance to treatment.

291. Trotter, Ann B.; Uhlig, George E.; and Fargo, Glenn. "Self-Actualization as a Predictor of Rehabilitation Counselor Success." *Rehabilitation Counseling Bulletin*, 15, 1 (September 1971): 58-67.

The relationship between counselor success and (a) experience as a rehabilitation counselor and (b) degree of self-actualization was studied. 21 rehabilitation counselors comprised the sample for this study. Success was measured by the percentage of rehabilitated case closure per case load. Self-actualization was assessed by 12 subscale scores on the Personal Orientation Inventory (POI). There was no relationship between counselor success and experience or any single subscale of the POI. A multiple linear regression indicated that the three best predictors of a counselor's success were (1) present oriented, (2) capacity for intimate contact, and (3) self-acceptance.

292. Tseng, M.S. "Predicting Vocational Rehabilitation Dropouts from Psychometric Attributes and Work Behavior." *Rehabilitation Counseling Bulletin*, 15, 3 (March 1972): 154-159.

11 instructors rated 142 clients on numerous psychometric measures and work behavior to assess what factors are associated with dropping out of a rehabilitation program. One-way variance analyses revealed that work behaviors and occupational interests differentiated between continuers and dropouts; IQ or cognitive skills did not.

293. Tseng, M.S. "Attitudes Toward the Disabled--A Cross-Cultural Study." *Journal of Social Psychology*, 87, 2 (August 1972): 311-312.

Using American and Asian students enrolled at an American university, this research seeks to answer: Would a cultural minority group show more positive attitudes toward the disabled than would a cultural majority group, due to sympathy for another minority? Or, would the cultural minority group show more negative attitudes toward the disabled than the cultural majority group, due to members' background in a traditional, less modern culture?

Overall, the Americans were more sympathetic than the Asians. Anxiety and length of time the Asian students stayed in the United States were significant correlates of attitude. Higher anxiety levels were associated with negative attitudes, and increased stay in the United States had a positive effect.

294. Tseng, M.S. "Job Performance and Satisfaction of Successfully Rehabilitated Vocational Rehabilitation Clients." *Rehabilitation Literature*, 36, 3 (March 1975): 66-72.

Occupational functioning of disabled employees who had been successfully rehabilitated by a state vocational rehabilitation agency and who were gainfully employed was investigated through the data collected from 65 such clients and 75 employers. While the employers as a group were considerably satisfied with their disabled employees in terms of work personality and proficiency and overall performance, the disabled employees themselves expressed moderately high degree of job satisfaction, attitude toward work, and self-acceptance. In comparison to their respective employer's ratings, the disabled clients tended to overestimate their own personal quality as measured by an 11-item work personality scale. Among the significant correlates of job satisfaction were work personality and self-acceptance. Self-acceptance proved to be a significant correlate of attitude toward work which was in turn significantly associated with spouse's conformity on family matters.

295. Tseng, M.S., and Zerega, W. Dennis. "The Intake Process and Outcome Performance of Vocational Rehabilitation in the Field." *Rehabilitation Literature*, 37, 11-12 (November-December 1976): 343-346.

14,569 clients served by the Division of Vocational Rehabilitation in an eastern state were examined. Factors associated with successful rehabilitation were: (1) being older, (2) having more dependents and earnings. Successful clients seem to receive significantly more expensive and concentrated training and services.

296. Turnbaugh, Karen; Guitar, Barry E.; and Hoffman, Paul R. "Speech Clinicians' Attributions of Personality

Traits as a Function of Stuttering Severity." *Journal of Speech and Hearing Research*, 22 (1979): 37-45.

36 speech-language pathologists rated individuals with different degrees of stuttering severity on a personality trait scale. The results indicated that the clinicians assigned negative personality traits to all levels of stuttering severity in comparison to normal individuals. Clinicians' ratings were not related to their professional experience. The implications of these findings are discussed with specific reference to how negative attitudes of clinicians may interfere with their ability to meet the needs of clients.

297. Udelman, Harold D., and Udelman, Mary Lou. "Group Therapy with Rheumatoid Arthritic Patients." *American Journal of Psychotherapy*, 32, 2 (April 1978): 288-299.

This report notes progress being made in a brief group psychotherapy program in an in-patient arthritis unit in Phoenix. Progress of four patients is detailed. Levels of group interaction are identified. They range from educative through exploratory-dynamic. Areas of discussion include: body image, family relationships, job status, and coping mechanisms. The authors suggest that a rheumatology group can help improve the responses of patients in in-patient medical treatment.

298. Ungar, Sheldon. "The Effects of Effort and Stigma on Helping." *Journal of Social Psychology*, 107, 1 (February 1979): 23-28.

This is a report of a field experiment performed on a subway platform. There were no differences in the help given to the stigmatized person wearing an eye patch and the nonstigmatized person in a low-effort condition, but the stigmatized were less likely to be helped than the nonstigmatized in the high-effort condition. The authors project that people often tend to avoid the handicapped. This avoidance is heightened if the situation has costs involved.

299. Van Demark, Duane R., and Van Demark, Ann A. "Speech and Socio-Vocational Aspects of Individuals with Cleft Palate." *Cleft Palate Journal*, 7, 1 (January 1970): 284-299.

A follow-up study of 39 patients born in 1946 and 1947, and admitted to University of Iowa Hospital, was conducted in the late 1960's. Male patients with cleft lip and palate were the group of patients with the poorest speech, while female patients with cleft lip and palate were the group with the lowest aesthetic rating. The average participation of the subjects in extracurricular activities was below the reported figure for high school graduates. Furthermore, those who participate in extracurricular activities tend to be observers, not activists.

300. Vernon, McCay, and Koh, Soon. "Early Manual Communication and Deaf Children's Achievement." *American Annals of the Deaf*, 115, 5 (September 1970): 527-536.

    This study compares the effects of early exposure to manual communication to early exposure to oral communication in genetically deaf children. Generally, support is offered for early manual communication. In particular, educational achievement and linguistic development were accelerated; speech and speech reading skills were not hurt by manual communication, and psychological adjustment is as good or better than in a comparison group. The author notes the gap between discovery of the value of the technique and its implementation in the field.

301. Vignos, P.J., Jr.; Thompson, H.M.; Katz, S.; Moskowitz, R.W.; Fink, S.; and Svec, K.H. "Comprehensive Care and Psychosocial Factors in Rehabilitation in Chronic Rheumatoid Arthritis: A Controlled Study." *Journal of Chronic Diseases*, 25 (1972): 457-467.

    This study investigated the factors associated with rehabilitation of 40 ambulatory patients with chronic severe rheumatoid arthritis one year after diagnosis. The findings indicated that there was no relationship between personal adjustment scores and improvement in activities of daily living. Patients with higher intelligence scores more often maintain functional performance and show greater improvement in social adjustment than patients with low intelligence scores. Improved social adjustment was seen more frequently in the intensive treatment group. The authors conclude that the findings support the idea that psychosocial factors are associated with rehabilitation measures, although they are not associated with the disease activity per se.

302. Vogel, Harvey D. "A Follow-Up Study of Former Student-Patients at the Crippled Children's Hospital and School, Sioux Falls, South Dakota." *Rehabilitation Literature*, 36 (September 1975): 270-273.

    A questionnaire follow-up study of orthopedically disabled patients was undertaken. 164 former patients who filled out all or part of the questionnaire become the sample for this study. The patients were divided into three groups: student, employer, and nonproductive.

When compared to the student and employed categories, the nonproductive group was more likely to be cerebral palsied, was less mobile, was less intelligent, achieved a lower level or education, was less apt to be married, participated less in social activities, was more apt to be living with parents, and was more physically disabled.

303. Von Isser, Aldine. "Psycholinguistic Abilities in Children with Epilepsy." *Exceptional Children*, 43, 5 (February 1977): 270-275.

50 epileptic children whose seizures were under control by medication were compared on the Illinois Test of Psycholinguistic Abilities with 50 control children. There were no significant differences between the two groups. There were also no significant differences within the epileptic group by type of seizure. The author argues that there is no necessity for special education provisions solely on the basis of diagnosis of epilepsy.

304. Voysey, Margaret. "Impression Management by Parents with Disabled Children." *Journal of Health and Social Behavior*, 13, 1 (March 1972): 80-89.

This study is based on a series of interviews with families of children recently diagnosed as having a "relatively severe" or "probably permanent" handicap. It documents the problems parents experience relative to the child's condition in encounters with persons outside the immediate family and the strategies adapted to manage such encounters. A typology of management is presented based on parents' responsibility and power. The researcher also probes the process of developing competence in interpersonal skills by parents of the disabled and how this affects the parents' identity and self-concept.

305. Wacker, Charles H. "Breaking the Competitive Employment Barrier for Blind People." *Journal of Rehabilitation*, 42, 3 (May-June 1976): 28-31, 40.

The author reports on the attitudes of seven major corporations toward hiring blind persons in competitive jobs. The report focuses on problems of communication, preconceptions, presentation, and credibility as experienced by both vocational counselors and blind applicants in open competitive markets.

306. Waechter, Eugenia H. "Children's Awareness of Fatal Illness." *American Journal of Nursing*, 71, 6 (June 1971): 1168-1172.

This study tests previous research findings that fatally ill children do not generally experience or express anxiety about death until they reach age 10. Four groups of children between the ages of 6 and 10 were tested on an anxiety scale and the TAT. Parents were also interviewed. Children with fatal illness scored twice as high on the anxiety scale as other hospitalized children. The make-up of stories as told by these children differed in theme from the comparison group. The fatally ill children emphasized death more. Also, their conversations stressed death, loneliness, and separation to a high degree. There was a sharp contrast between the parents' perception of the child's awareness of condition and prognosis and the child's knowledge. The researcher concludes that in their protected environments terminally ill children may not express directly their fears and awareness of their illness, but given a chance to do so indirectly, they express these fears and their knowledge.

307. Walls, Richard T.; Miller, John J.; and Cox, Janet. "Delay of Reinforcement and Training Choice Behavior for Rehabilitation Clients." *Rehabilitation Counseling Bulletin*, 14, 2 (December 1970): 69-77.

132 clients in various job skill training programs at the West Virginia Rehabilitation Center comprised the sample for the study. Levels of salary and length of training were varied to assess the training choice behavior of clients. Findings were as follows:
(1) Clients will defer immediate, less valued employment for a better job after training.
(2) The willingness to enter a training program decreases as the training period lengthens.
(3) Internal control clients were more willing to be trained than external control clients.

308. Wan, Thomas T.H. "Correlates and Consequences of Severe Disabilities." *Journal of Occupational Medicine*, 16, 4 (April 1974): 234-244.

The author proposes a causal model of disability that consists of three types of factors: agent, host, and environmental. Agent factors include: disabling conditions, length of disability, and secondary impairments. Host factors include: education, occupation, age, sex, and race. Environmental factors include: industry, poverty status, and migration-residence status. The data used is from the 1967 Survey of Economic Opportunity. The three factors are said to exert an independent influence on the risk of being severely disabled. Industry, length of disability, and poverty status are viewed as most important. Host and environmental factors are most important in determining propensity to work full time. Agent factors and severity of disability did not seem to exert an influence. Earnings are most affected by the disabling attributes which limit work capacity and employability.

309. Ward, Allen L. "The Response of Individuals Beginning Work with Blind Persons." *New Outlook for the Blind*, 67, 1 (January 1973): 1-5.

This study reports on interviews with 90 interns concerning their reactions to working with blind persons for the first time. Persons with previous contacts experienced depression, frustration, fear, sorrow, pity, revulsion, guilt, and resentment intensely for a short time and less so for a longer period. It is suggested that persons entering such situations be forewarned and that individual and group counseling can be helpful.

310. Weinberg-Asher, Nancy. "The Effect of Physical Disability on Self-Perception." *Rehabilitation Counseling Bulletin*, 20, 1 (September 1976): 15-20.

This study investigated the hypothesis that the physically disabled devalued themselves because they were not physically able. The sample consisted of 139 rehabilitation students at a special summer program at the University of Illinois. A comparison group of able-bodied students matched on sex and year in school was secured. A self-description questionnaire was used. There were no significant differences between the two groups of students. Sex differences were noted, but there was no sex and physical condition interaction found. The author argues that these findings question the majority view that the physically disabled introject society's view of them as different. The author recognizes that the college student sample may be atypical.

311. Weinberg, Nancy. "Preschool Children's Perceptions of Orthopedic Disability." *Rehabilitation Counseling Bulletin*, 21, 3 (March 1978): 183-189.

This research investigated whether attitudes toward a disabled child differ among preschoolers. Photographs were used as the stimuli and the sample consisted of 25 able-bodied three year olds, 53 four year olds, and 23 five year olds. Findings indicated that understanding of disability did not occur until four years of age. Ratings of photographs on social indicators revealed no differences in selection of able-bodied children as compared to disabled children. When measured in relation with whom to play, the subjects selected the able-bodied students significantly more often. The author reasons that preschool education should focus on attitudes toward the physically disabled before such attitudes become set.

312. Weinberg, Nancy. "Modifying Social Stereotypes of the Physically Disabled." *Rehabilitation Counseling Bulletin*, 22, 2 (December 1978): 114-124.

The present research examined whether perceptions of the disabled are affected by contact with the disabled. In Experiment #1, the attitudes of elementary school age students in a segregated school vs. a mainstreamed school were examined. In Experiment #2 the attitudes of college students living in a segregated dormitory, an integrated dormitory, and an integrated room were examined. The ratings consisted of 26 descriptive items such as "a good person" to "is selfish" for the stimuli (pictured child). The results of Experiment #1 indicated that there was a differential perception of the disabled by the students and there were no differences between the segregated and mainstreamed students. The results of Experiment #2 indicated that there was a differential perception of the disabled by the students and the degree of difference between abled and disabled was a function of degree of contact between both groups. The integrated roommate had the smallest difference, whereas the segregated one had the most. The results of these studies suggest that only in situations in which very extensive and intimate contact occur are the disabled seen as fairly similar to the able-bodied.

313. Weinberg, Nancy, and Williams, Judy. "How the Physically Disabled Perceive Their Disabilities." *Journal of Rehabilitation*, 44, 3 (July-September 1978): 31-33.

This study reports on a questionnaire survey of 88 individuals with various kinds of physical disabilities. At least 64% of the respondents felt that their disability was an at least somewhat important characteristic about themselves. However, only a small percentage thought of their disability as either a terrible thing or the worst thing that ever happened to them. Most viewed their disability as a fact of life or an inconvenience. Respondents were evenly distributed about whether or not they would wish their disability away. Respondents were also evenly distributed in feelings about whether their disability had advantages. The most commonly cited advantage was that disability provided a goal or purpose to work toward. Overall, the disabled did not view their condition as a great tragedy.

314. Weinberg, Nancy, and Santana, Rosina. "Comic Books: Champions of the Disabled Stereotype." *Rehabilitation Literature*, 39, 11-12 (November/December 1978): 327-331.

Content analysis technique was used to assess whether comic books present a stereotypical image of the physically different. 40 comic books were sampled. The findings indicated that the physically disabled were represented as either good or evil. There were no average or ordinary, yet physically different, figures. This misrepresentation of the physically different makes it more difficult for the disabled to be accepted as persons who happen to be disabled.

315. Wendland, Carroll J. "Internal-External Control Expectancies of Institutionalized Physically Disabled." *Rehabilitation Psychology*, 20, 3 (Winter 1973): 180-186.

This study examines developmental consequences of institutional living. Chronicity of disability and percentage of time institutionalized since onset of disability were examined in relation to the internal-external control expectancies of physically disabled men. The proportion of time institutionalized was not significantly related to control expectancies; chronicity of disability was a more important variable. Patients disabled less than a year and a half had much higher external scores than those disabled three years or more. The finding suggests that the period follow-

ing onset of disability is marked by expectations of
increased direction from external forces.

316. Wendland, Leonard V. "The Measuring of Patient Cooperativeness." *Rehabilitation Psychology*, 20, 3 (Fall 1973): 121-125.

It is generally assumed that in order for rehabilitation to be successful, both patients and staff must enter into a climate of cooperation. Failure or unplanned outcomes are sometimes termed "not cooperative." This paper reports on three scales that allow the quantification of patient behaviors that are related to cooperativeness. The scale items were contributed by workers in the field and submitted to the Thurstone scaling techniques. The study proposes three scales of 30 items each of which are assumed to measure cooperative-uncooperative behavior. Such scales should allow diagnosis of patients as good or poor candidates for rehabilitation. They should also suggest which behaviors need to be modified for rehabilitation to take place.

317. Wiener, Carolyn L. "The Burden of Rheumatoid Arthritis: Tolerations the Uncertainty." *Social Science and Medicine*, 9, 2 (February 1975): 97-104.

Through observation and interview material this study reports on the management of daily activities by individuals with rheumatoid arthritis. Emphasis is on uncertainty on a day-to-day basis and the variables that produce uncertainty as well as the social strategies of normalizing, covering-up, keeping up, and pacing. Description is offered on how arthritics balance strategies available to them. Also, the author offers a short comparative discussion of arthritics versus sufferers from other diseases, such as colitis and emphysema, in terms of managing uncertainties.

318. Wilson, Earl D. "A Comparison of the Effects of Deafness Simulation and Observation upon Attitudes, Anxiety, and Behavior Manifested Toward the Deaf." *Journal of Special Education*, 5 (Winter 1971): 343-349.

Students in beginning classes in educational psychology were randomly assigned to three conditions: deafness simulation, observation, and controls. Attitude Toward Deaf Persons Scale and the Semantic-Differential

Scale were administered. Following the experimental condition, the deafness simulation group rated the deaf lower on the Semantic-Differential ratings of self and of persons who are deaf than did the other two groups. Other findings were not significant.

319. Wirls, Charles, and Plotkin, Rosalie R. "A Comparison of Children with Cleft Palate and Their Siblings in Projective Test Personality Factors." *Cleft Palate Journal*, 8, 4 (December 1971): 399-408.

66 children with cleft lip and/or palate who were between the ages of 7 and 14 years and who had a non-cleft sibling in this age range were studied on several subjective measures of personality adjustment. The number of significant differences between the two groups were less than expected by chance. These results support the premise that there is no specific personality type associated with this particular handicap.

320. Woods, C. Lee. "Social Position and Speaking Competence of Stuttering and Normally Fluent Boys." *Journal of Speech and Hearing Research*, 17, 4 (December 1974): 740-747.

Ratings of social position and speaking competence were obtained for 24 boys who stutter (12 mild and 12 moderate or severe) and from 562 of their normally fluent male classmates. No significant differences between groups of boys who stutter were found on peer ratings and ratings of self-esteem. Except for speech competence, there were no significant differences between those boys with fluency and stuttering on social position measures. Findings support the idea that stuttering at an elementary school age level does not influence the child's social role among his peers.

321. Woods, C.L., and Williams, D.E. "Speech Clinicians' Conceptions of Boys and Men who Stutter." *Journal of Speech and Hearing Disorders*, 36, 2 (May 1971): 225-234.

Presented in the study are speech clinicians' conceptions of "what stutterers are like." The authors' investigation of the connotative aspects of the term "stutterer" was accomplished by having speech clinicians write adjectives they felt best described the adult stutterer. Their responses were compared with

the same information obtained about elementary-school-
aged boys who stutter. The authors found many of the
same adjectives listed for both men and boys, indicating a fairly well-established stereotype of a stutterer
regardless of age. When adjectives were grouped into
broad behavior categories, approximately 75% of the
clinicians listed adjectives within the category "nervous or fearful," and 64% listed those that were in
the category of "shy and insecure." Only 31% of the
clinicians listed adjectives that reflected "abnormalities of speech." The author feels that the results
of this study should be of great interest for all clinicians working with persons who stutter and particularly those who sit for the first time across the clinical desk and begin to work with a stutterer.

322. Woods, C. Lee, and Williams, Dean E. "Traits Attributed to Stuttering and Normally Fluent Males."
Journal of Speech and Hearing Research, 19, 2 (June
1976): 267-278.

156 adults with differing degree of familiarity and
experience with stuttering rated four hypothetical
situations comparing stuttering and fluent boys and
men on 25 scales arranged in a semantic differential
format. Findings indicated that the persons who stutter were rated as unfavorable and that this rating is
unaffected by the amount of exposure to actual stutterers. Individuals need help to handle this initial reaction to their speech.

323. Woo-Sam, James; Zimmerman, Irla Lee; Brunk, Joyce D.;
Uyehara, Katherine; and Miller, Allan R. "Socio-
Economic Status and Post-Trauma Intelligence in Children with Severe Head Injuries." *Psychological Reports*, 27 (1970): 147-153.

46 patients with severe head injuries were studied
to assess the degree of intellectual recovery post-
trauma. Recovery was best predicted by age, with older
children (10 years or older) scoring higher than younger children. Results were independent of the socioeconomic status of the subjects.

324. Wright, Edwin T.; Kyle, N.L.; and Gunter, R. "Personality Test Configurations in Acne Vulgaries." *Perceptual and Motor Skills*, 30 (February 1970): 191-
201.

52 college female students, whose age averaged 20 years, were clinically divided into two groups according to the severity of their acne. All 52 subjects were administered a battery of psychological tests including the MMPI. It was found that the MMPI Scale score significantly differentiated between groups with acne and no acne, as well as between groups with mild and severe acne. The group with mild acne showed improvement in their MMPI scores one year later, after having lessons in skin treatment, whereas the group with severe acne did not. The authors concluded that the findings supported the notion that personality differences exist between sufferers with mild and severe acne.

325. Wright, Edwin T.; Martin, Rose; Flynn, Catherine; and Gunter, Ralph. "Some Psychological Effects of Cosmetics." *Perceptual and Motor Skills*, 30 (February 1970): 12-14.

This study reported the results of pre- and post-tests designed to assess the effects of cosmetics on the self-concept of 42 college girls with various degrees of facial blemishes which could not be improved by better hygiene. For three months the subjects received weekly instruction in the use of cosmetics. The subjects were pre- and post-tested with the MMPI, especially the D scale (depression) and the Pt scale (psychasthenia). On both scales, the subjects scored significantly higher on the post-tests, indicating improvement in these areas. The authors argue that the correct use of cosmetics resulted in the higher scores.

326. Wright, V., and Owen, S. "The Effect of Rheumatoid Arthritis on the Social Situation of Housewives." *Rheumatology and Rehabilitation*, 15, 3 (August 1976): 156-160.

Emphasis in this report is on the husband's reactions to his wife's rheumatoid arthritis. Most patients understood and accepted the disease themselves. In 70% of the cases it was felt that the husbands understood the disease, but that half of the wives experienced difficulty in coping with their husbands' anxiety about the disease. Patients who developed the disease before marriage seemed to fare better in terms of understanding, guilt, adjustment, husband's understanding, and friction in the home. Patients with a milder disease were themselves more anxious, but experienced greater understanding from the spouse. Discussion centers on the type of patient for whom help in coping seems most appropriate.

327. Wrzesniewski, Kazimierz. "The Attitudes Toward the Illness of Patients after Myocardial Infarction Undergoing Rehabilitation." *Social Science and Medicine*, 9, 4/5 (April/May 1975): 237-239.

This study examines attitudes of 160 males toward myocardial infarction and the relationship between these attitudes and undergoing rehabilitation. All subjects were in a rehabilitation sanitarium and all suffered their first myocardial infarction. Organized comprehensive rehabilitation affected attitudes positively. Attitudes favorable toward the course of treatment are identified.

328. Yairs, Ehud, and Williams, Dean E. "Reports of Parental Attitudes by Stuttering and Nonstuttering Children." *Journal of Speech and Hearing Research*, 14, 3 (September 1971): 596-604.

34 boys who stutter (17 mild and 17 moderate-severe) and 34 boys who do not stutter, all in the sixth and seventh grades of school, completed the Children's Report of Parent Behavior Inventory. The boys who stutter tended to view their parents as behaving with less control and hostility and with more love and autonomy than did the boys who do not stutter. The degree of stuttering was not a factor in determining reported parental behavior. The authors conclude that the premise that parent-child problems are a factor in etiology of stuttering is not supported by the findings of this study.

329. Yelin, Edward H.; Feshbach, Dan M.; Meenan, Robert F.; and Epstein, Wallace V. "Social Problems, Services and Policy for Persons with Chronic Disease: The Case of Rheumatoid Arthritis." *Social Science and Medicine*, 13C, 2 (March 1979): 13-20.

Interviews were conducted with 50 persons with arthritis to determine the medical and social costs of their condition. Interviewers also provided information on the utilization of social and medical services. Data indicates that income losses greatly exceed medical costs, but that persons with rheumatoid arthritis utilize medical services more frequently than social services. Discussion is offered relative to increasing social service utilization and policy questions.

330. Zahn, Margaret H. "Incapacity, Impotence and Invisible Impairment: Their Effects upon Interpersonal Relations." *Journal of Health and Social Behavior*, 14, 2 (June 1973): 115-123.

This study assesses the influence of certain characteristics of impairments upon a variety of interpersonal relations. The interpersonal relations examined include relations with spouse, general family relations, relations with friends, and casual secondary encounters. The characteristics of impairment examined include: severity of impairment, kind of functional limitations associated with the impairment, and visibility of the impairment.

Data is drawn from randomly selected applicants for disability benefits in the New Orleans, Minneapolis-St. Paul, and Columbus, Ohio, areas. The subjects include 1,024 individuals judged severely disabled and 244 persons judged totally disabled. A variety of disorders are included, e.g., circulatory, musculoskeletal, neurological, respiratory. Data is obtained through interviews with subjects by a clinical team and combined with medical and clinical evaluations and laboratory tests.

The severely impaired are likely to have better interpersonal relations than are the less severely impaired. Impairment that results in loss of communication skills will be very disabling in all interpersonal relations with secondary relationships being most affected. Fitness to work was positively linked with interpersonal relations and this relationship held more clearly for males than females. However, it did not hold for conjugal and family relationships. In close primary relationships where individuals are judged fit to work but are not working, there is the most negative impact on interpersonal relationships. The sexually impaired have better relationships with their spouses and suffer less disruption in general family relations than do the nonimpaired.

Findings related to communication, work, and sexual capacities indicate that some kinds of functional limitations, but not all, do make a difference in interpersonal relations between the physically impaired and the nonimpaired.

The kind of functional limitations that seem most problematic are those that create an ambiguous status for the person or hamper the ability to clarify his or her status.

This study also examined the visibility of impairment, i.e., presence of equipment for ambulation or muscular support. Visibility was as disruptive of conjugal and family relations as of secondary relationships, but no more disruptive for young than for old. In all social classes, the visibly impaired reported more disruption than the nonimpaired, but there were no class differences.

In general, characteristics of impairment that clearly indicate sickness or impairment tend to be associated with better interpersonal relationships. The study does not support those label theorists who feel that indications of impairment will lead to a definition as deviant. Rather it indicates that a clear label may lead to greater self-acceptance and a subsequent social acceptance.

JOURNALS SEARCHED
(Unless noted otherwise, search covers
the period 1970-1979 inclusive.)

Ambulatory Pediatrics
American Annals of the Deaf
American Archives of Rehabilitation Therapy
American Foundation of Blind Research Bulletin (discontinued
    June 1975)
American Journal of Diseases of Children
American Journal of Nursing
American Journal of Orthopsychiatry
American Journal of Psychiatry
American Journal of Psychotherapy
American Journal of Public Health
American Journal of Sociology
American Review of Respiratory Diseases
American Sociological Review
Annals of Physical Medicine (title changed to Rheumatology
    and Physical Medicine in August 1970, and then to Rheu-
    matology and Rehabilitation in February 1973)
Archives of Diseases of Children
Archives of General Psychiatry
Archives of Physical Medicine
Artificial Limbs
Behavioral Therapy
British Journal of Disorders of Communication
British Journal of Medical Psychology
British Journal of Psychiatry
British Journal of Psychology
British Medical Journal
Canadian Journal of Behavioral Science
Canadian Welfare
Child Development
Child Psychiatry and Human Development
Child Study Journal
Childhood Education
Children (titled changed to Children Today in January 1972)
Cleft Palate Journal

Clinical Genetics
Clinical Pediatrics
Community Health (discontinued in May 1978)
Developmental Medicine and Child Neurology
Epilepsia
Exceptional Children
Exceptional Parent (Volume 1 began June 1971)
Health and Social Work (Volume 1 began April 1976)
Human Relations
Illinois Medical Journal
Journal of Abnormal Psychology
Journal of Applied Behavior Analysis
Journal of Applied Psychology
Journal of Behavior Therapy and Experimental Psychology
Journal of Child Psychiatry
Journal of Child Psychology
Journal of Chronic Diseases
Journal of Consulting and Clinical Psychology
Journal of Educational Psychology
Journal of Exceptional Children
Journal of Genetic Psychology
Journal of Health and Social Behavior
Journal of Learning Disabilities
Journal of Marriage and the Family
Journal of Occupational Medicine
Journal of Pediatrics
Journal of Personality and Social Psychology
Journal of Psychology
Journal of Rehabilitation
Journal of Rehabilitation for the Deaf
Journal of School Psychology
Journal of Social Issues
Journal of Social Psychology
Journal of Special Education
Journal of Speech and Hearing Disorders
Journal of Speech and Hearing Research
Lancet
Medical Clinics of North America
Mental Hygiene (discontinued in Fall 1977)
Merrill Palmer Quarterly
Milbank Memorial Fund Quarterly
Monthly Labor Review
New England Journal of Medicine
New Outlook for the Blind (title changed to Journal of Visual
    Impairment and Blindness in January 1977)
Nursing Research
Pacific Sociological Review

Peabody Journal of Education
Pediatric Clinics of North America
Pediatric Research
Perceptual and Motor Skills
Personnel and Guidance Journal
Plastic and Reconstructive Surgery
Psychological Forschung (title changed to Psychological Research in 1975)
Psychological Reports
Psychosomatics
Rehabilitation Counseling Bulletin
Rehabilitation Literature
Rehabilitation Psychology (discontinued after Volume 21, Number 4, 1974)
Scandinavian Journal of Rehabilitative Medicine
Social Casework
Social Forces
Social Problems
Social Science in Medicine
Social Service Review
Social Work
Social Work in Health Care (Volume 1 began Fall 1975)
Sociological Inquiry
Sociology of Education
Teacher of the Deaf (title changed to British Association of Teachers of the Deaf in January 1977)
Volta Review

SUBJECT INDEX

Academic achievement 2, 3, 9, 56, 67, 82, 105, 123, 192, 210, 215, 237, 259, 271, 288, 300
Acceptance of disability
    by others 6, 7, 9, 27, 30, 67, 88, 104, 293
    by self 4, 16, 117, 158, 163, 190, 268, 286, 294, 306, 310, 313, 315, 327
Adolescence and adjustment to disability 58, 65, 92, 93, 121, 166, 179, 190, 197, 212, 275, 276, 279
Age
    as a factor in defining "handicapped" 41
    as a factor in rehabilitation 28, 31, 52, 62, 76, 87, 90, 91, 107, 112, 121, 123, 132, 133, 141, 161, 194, 201, 203, 207, 208, 222, 295
Amputee 34, 286
Anxiety 167, 172, 293
Apgar Scale 262
Aphasia 164
Arthritic disorders 70, 169, 297, 301, 317, 326, 329
Articulation disorders 101, 184
Asthma 192, 229
Attitude Toward Disabled Persons Scale 54, 64, 81, 149, 167, 250, 268, 272
Attitudes
    change of 54, 64, 148, 149, 174, 225, 245, 248, 312, 318
    of handicapped toward handicapped 47, 63, 151, 211, 285
    of handicapped toward normals 47
    of handicapped toward staff 36, 111, 285, 310
    hierarchical structure of 63, 99, 104, 118, 122, 130, 199, 205, 211, 231-233, 253, 254, 257, 285, 289
    measurement of 95, 311, 316
    of normals toward handicapped 71, 72, 89, 108, 122, 127, 130, 151, 167, 172, 211, 231, 236, 254, 293, 298, 305, 309, 312, 314, 318, 322
    of staff toward handicapped 46, 53, 60, 98, 99, 111, 118, 131, 137, 146, 150, 176, 177, 199, 223, 257, 283, 296, 309, 321
Awareness of terminal illness 96, 306

Bayley Scale 262, 277
Behavioral adjustment 70, 82, 102, 107, 184, 206, 210, 228, 237, 239, 275
Behavioral mapping 189
Behavioral modification 17, 83, 284, 307
Birth order 78
Black lung 11
Blind 9, 12, 13, 17, 26, 67, 72, 83, 86, 87, 106, 115, 131, 140, 147, 152, 155, 165-167, 176, 177, 181, 197, 210, 255, 271, 298, 305, 309
Boehm Test of Basic Concepts 56
Brain injured 5, 90, 261, 288, 323
Breast augmentation 266
Burn injury 92, 170, 223

Camping 60, 74
Cancer 96, 153, 213, 256, 273
Cerebral palsy 20, 110, 137, 162, 190, 209, 250, 302
Cerebrovascular accidents (see Stroke)
Children's reactions
  handicapped children to other children 2, 18, 232
  handicapped children to self 15, 218, 287, 306
  normal children to the handicapped 18, 30, 74, 106, 124, 129, 148, 182, 218, 225, 234, 236, 252, 253, 311, 320
Cleft lip and/or palate 27, 38, 55, 68, 77, 82, 89, 126, 142, 146, 156, 183-185, 214-217, 237, 238-240, 259, 270, 274-277, 299, 319
Client change 24
Client knowledge 66
Communication problems
  client-provider 36
  and the deaf 112, 168, 300
  language disorders 69, 88, 101, 222, 269, 303
  parent-staff 20
Coronary heart disease and personality traits 120, 173, 202, 265
Cystic fibrosis 93, 280, 290

Denial 34, 50, 59, 128, 139, 153, 200
Diabetes 66, 212
Dialysis (see Renal dialysis)
Disability, measurement of 100, 138, 272
Dysmorphogenesis 82

Education as a factor in rehabilitation (see Social class)
Employability of handicapped 7, 8, 12, 22, 23, 32, 33, 52, 57, 58, 81, 84, 90-94, 97, 108-110, 133, 141, 143, 159, 162, 185, 201, 207, 216, 219, 220, 224, 226, 242, 248, 257, 279, 292, 294, 295, 299, 302, 305, 307, 308

Epidemiology of disability   201
Epilepsy   61, 62, 105, 107, 174, 188, 224, 248, 303
Esophageal speech   88, 132
Ethnicity   145
Exposure as a variable in reaction toward handicapped   67, 127, 131, 140, 146, 254, 272

Facial disfigurement   7, 19, 92, 238, 268
Family impact   55, 65, 79, 80, 139, 147, 164, 168, 170, 171, 178, 179, 200, 213, 227, 246, 249, 281, 290, 294, 302, 319, 326, 330

Geographic location as a factor in reaction to handicapped   40
Group therapy   16, 36, 51, 85, 110, 165, 166, 258, 280, 297

Handicapped, definition of   40
Hearing impaired   10, 21-23, 33, 44, 45, 53, 56, 79, 112, 121, 125, 134, 135, 141, 163, 168, 195, 219, 220, 226-228, 251, 279, 300, 318
Heart patients   48, 50, 108, 120, 153, 157, 173, 194
Heart surgery   28, 29, 143
Helping patterns   9, 49, 70, 247, 267, 298
Hemiplegics   14
Hemophilia   246
Hospitalization effects   274
Housing preferences of handicapped   43
Hypertension   114
Hypnosis   54

Intellectual functioning   44, 45, 56, 61, 62, 68, 107, 121, 125, 133, 142, 152, 155, 156, 162, 183, 224, 227, 238, 259, 262, 264, 277, 292, 301, 302, 323

Knowledge as a factor in rehabilitation   66, 88, 187, 200

Labeling   154
Laryngectomy   88, 91, 132
Learning disability   30, 35, 103
Leprosy   19
Lesion level   119
Leukemia   85
Limb loss   4
Lisping   198
Locus of control   21, 27, 35, 287, 307, 315
Longitudinal studies   86, 104, 124, 129, 135, 137, 191, 208, 213, 224, 244, 260, 265, 277, 278, 302

Mainstreaming   30, 60, 67, 106, 134, 135, 163, 181, 227, 236, 251-253, 255

Marital status as a factor in rehabilitation 52, 91, 161, 162
Memory 44
Minnesota Multiphasic Personality Inventory (MMPI) 31, 75, 132, 188, 264, 273, 278, 324, 325
Misdiagnosis 10
Mode of address 25
Morale 29
Mother's attitudes 35, 38
Motor skill 5
Multiple sclerosis 175, 284
Myklebust Picture Story Language Test 68
Myocardial infarction 16, 50, 84, 109, 117, 178, 202, 263, 327

Nasality 18, 89
Neurological disorders 7, 221

Occupational goals 115
Orthodontic rehabilitation 244
Orthopedic rehabilitation 97, 123, 124, 240, 311

Paraplegia 204, 206
Parental expectations 2, 105, 137, 191, 239, 288, 304, 328
Patient satisfaction 25
Personality
    characteristics of disabled 21, 29, 59, 126, 157, 161, 173, 256, 261, 291, 316, 319, 324
    as a factor in rehabilitation 24, 57, 128, 222
Physical attractiveness 1, 2, 39, 74, 92, 144, 145, 172, 182, 230, 282, 324, 325
Physical functioning 3, 109, 119, 157
PKU 193
Predicting rehabilitation outcomes 14, 23, 75, 159, 243, 273, 292
Psychological adjustment 79, 136, 139, 196, 200, 206, 221, 246, 260, 261, 270, 278, 290, 301, 325
Punishment-and-reward approach 17

Quadriplegia 245, 284
Quay and Peterson Behavior Checklist 102, 228, 237, 239

Race
    as a factor in attitudes 1, 129, 234
    as a factor in rehabilitation success 52, 114, 141, 201, 203
Rehabilitation success 3, 8, 11, 13, 22, 23, 52, 57, 76, 84, 87, 161, 187, 209, 283, 291, 292, 294, 295, 301, 308, 330

Subject Index

Religion
    as a factor in reaction to handicapped 40
    as a factor in rehabilitation 48
Renal dialysis 31, 51, 57-59, 94, 113, 249, 281
Renal transplants 15, 136, 139
Retinoblastoma 155
Rheumatic fever 278

Scoliosis 200
Self-concept 117, 126, 136, 153, 158, 175, 186, 193, 195,
    202, 204, 244, 251, 268, 269, 271, 275, 287, 310, 320
Sex
    of patient as a factor in rehabilitation 28, 52, 76, 91,
        121, 125, 142, 159, 161, 201, 203, 241, 268, 270
    in reaction to handicapped 1, 2, 9, 40, 41, 46, 150
Sexuality among handicapped 73, 160
Sick role 3, 28, 57, 59, 78, 116, 194
Similarity attraction model 6
Social class as a factor in rehabilitation 70, 84, 103, 114,
    141, 161, 180, 192, 194, 201, 203, 207, 208, 210, 242,
    255, 263, 323
Social functioning 2, 3, 19, 91, 96, 102, 105, 107, 113, 123,
    136, 143, 185, 206, 214, 215, 217, 255, 326, 330
Sociometric studies 74, 106, 134, 135, 232, 235, 236
Spina bifida 5, 65, 80, 171, 179
Spinal-cord-injured patients 37, 119, 133, 196, 204
Stigma management 34, 304
Stroke 36, 153, 159, 186
Stuttering 222, 269, 296, 320-322, 328

Teacher attitudes 1, 42, 98, 99, 131, 140, 150, 205, 211,
    230, 238, 239
Tolerance of ambiguity 128, 317

Verbal stimulation 21, 45
Visual rehabilitation 13, 106, 154, 165, 181, 243
Vocational rehabilitation (see Employability of handicapped)

Wechsler Intelligence Scale 61, 62, 69, 76, 203, 264

INDEX OF SECOND AUTHORS

Acheson, Roy M.   70
Adelson, Ruth   225
Ahmadian, Seyed   136
Allen, Harry A.   73
Alston, Paul P.   53

Baylor, J.   12
Beach, Dorothy   207, 208
Bernstein, Norman R.   92, 223
Bigwood, A. Winton   94
Birch, Jack   210
Blumin, Shirley S.   287
Boder, Karl F.   266
Boersma, Frederick   35
Bohman, M.   107
Broman, Sarah H.   262
Brooks, Nancy A.   175
Brookshire, Bonnie   77
Bruininks, Robert H.   134
Brunk, Joyce D.   323
Burns, Ivan K.   193
Buschman, Penelope R.   85
Byrd, Dianne   32

Canter, Harry   277
Carey, Richard   225
Chadwick, O.F.D.   261
Chagoya, L.   260
Chalfant, Anna Lee   66
Cherry, Thomas   212
Chinsky, Rosalie R.   214-217, 277
Cleveland, G.L.   120
Clifford, Edward   27
Cohen, Shirley   129
Cohn, George   281
Cole, Roberta C.   66

Conire, Tali   272
Connolly, M. Estelle   146
Cox, Janet   307
Creer, Thomas L.   229
Crocker, Eleanor C.   38
Croke, Katherine   225
Croog, Sydney H.   117
Crosby, Roberta   92
Czackes, J.W.   59

Danzer, Claus   259
Davis, John E., Jr.   196
Davis, R.M.   286
Davison, B.   192
Demos, G.D.   149, 151
Dilgard, Victor W.   290
Diller, Leonard   14
Donahue, Elizabeth M.   66
Donnelly, E.F.   188
Doolan, Susan J.   198
Downs, A. Chris   144
Dudovitz, Dorothy   280
Duehn, Wayne D.   177
Dunn, Marilyn   158
Dunn, Michael   37
Dyck, Norma   211

Edwards, Larry   272
Emener, William G.   32
Emerson, Patricia   234
Epstein, Wallace V.   329
Ewert, J.C.   132

Fargo, Glenn   291
Feigenbaum, Helen   281
Feinberg, Lawrence   81
Feshbach, Dan M.   329

Fine, Richard N.   139
Fink, S.   301
Finkelstein, Frederic   281
Finnie, Nancie R.   20
Fisher, Mary J.   216, 217
Flowers, C.R.   132
Flynn, Catherine   325
Fogel, Max L.   43
Frank, Charles W.   263
Franklin, Susan   66
Franz, Martha Neal   290
Friedman, Matthew J.   235
Friedman, Stanford B.   200

Gaines, L.   151
Gardner, James E.   139
Garn, S.M.   82
Garner, Ann   212
Gasperini, Richard M.   146
Gensley, J.T.   148
Gerstman, Louis   14
Getsinger, Stephen H.   46
Goddard, Dorothy Rose   86
Granich, Bell   246
Graves, William, III   138
Green, J.B.   105
Griner, Gene Gary   204
Grushken, Carl M.   139
Gugely, K. Ted   19
Guitar, Barry E.   296
Gunter, Ralph   324, 325

Haas, Albert   14
Hackett, J.D.   191
Hackett, Thomas P.   16
Hagan, Frank   283
Hakmiller, Karl L.   119
Hambleton, Donald   227
Harley, J.P.   62
Harper, Dennis   240
Harper, Mary   82
Harris, Mary B.   247
Hastings, Jane O.   79
Haug, Marie R.   283
Hayward, James R.   82
Heim, Ruth E.   83
Heimburger, Richard E.   270
Heiserman, Kitty   276

Herndon, Charles H.   136
Hickok, Nell   66
Higgins, Paul C.   3
Hilgartner, Margaret   246
Hochman, M.E.   286
Hoffman, Paul R.   296
Hohman, George W.   196
Holman, Barbara L.   114
Horne, Marcia D.   104
Houldin, B.   227
Huttner, Muriel   69
Hyman, Melvin   18

Iker, H.   256
Ishida, Dianne N.   66
Isralsky, M.   93

Jaffe, Yoram   4
Janzen, Frederick V.   161
Johansen, Norma   162
Johns, Jeannie   21
Jones, Reginald L.   197
Jorgensen, Gary O.   161

Kappes, Bruno M.   98
Katz, Irwin   129
Katz, Shlomo   251, 301
Keith, Robert Allen   189
Kelz, James W.   159, 167
Keogh, Barbara K.   103
Killou, D.   191
Kimball, Bud D.   69
Kitsen, Jenny   281
Kitson, Gary C.   283
Kjellman, Anna Malmer   90
Klech, Robert E.   236
Koh, Soon   300
Koppes, Bruno M.   211
Kucharis, Sue   166
Kunce, Joseph T.   46, 257
Kunishi, Marilyn M.   66
Kyle, N.L.   324

Lana, Robert H.   186
Langlois, Judith H.   282
Larson, Janet   10
Latz, Adolph   52
LaVoie, Joseph C.   2

Index of Second Authors

Lawrence, Lorraine 36
Lebouits, B.Z. 265
Leeper, Herbert A. 142
Levine, Sol 48-50, 117
Levitt, Marc 155
Lewis, Sally C. 104
Lindholm, Byron W. 288
Lipson, Alberta 49
Lomranz, Jacob 4
Lynch, Joan 77

MacDonald, Robert W. 113
Macintyre, Mary M.J. 202
MacQueen, John C. 278
Malkin, Susan F. 79
Malone, Marquette S. 164
Martin, Rose 325
Martinson, Melton C. 64
Matthews, C.G. 61, 62
Matthews, Hannah P. 183
Matthews, Sharon J. 182
Mayerovitch, J. 260
McCauley, Robert 135
McGurn, Welatha C. 96
McLelland, P. 12
McWilliams, Betty Jane 68
Meenan, Robert F. 329
Meier, Joseph 277
Mercer, Ann S. 139
Miller, Alan R. 323
Miller, John 195
Miller, John J. 307
Morin, S. 160
Moskowitz, R.W. 301
Musgrave, Ross H. 184

Negrete, Vida F. 139
Newman, Joseph 11
Northcott, Winifred 135
Nugent, Lynn H. 66
Nystrom, John B. 162

O'Donnell, John M. 266
Oglesby, P. 265
Orpet, Russell E. 148, 149
Orth, Donald 109
Ostfeld, A.M. 65

Overberger, James E. 146
Owen, S. 326

Paradise, Leon P. 185
Parrioh, Thomas S. 98
Pedersen, Susan 280
Pellegrini, Ronald V. 143
Penta, Frank B. 245
Permenter, N.A. 12
Persons, Roy W. 284
Peterson, J. 218
Piliavin, June A. 47
Plaisted, Sally 66
Plewis, Ian 5
Plotkin, Rosalie R. 319
Pollak, Otto 96
Ptacek, Paul H. 164

Rahe, R.H. 157
Rawlinson, May 28, 29
Reitz, Joseph 9
Richardson, Stephen A. 74
Robinson, John F. 202
Robson, Richard 109
Rodin, Ernest A. 224
Rogers, D. 151
Ronald, Linda 74, 236
Roseman, R.H. 120
Rosenbaum, Arthur L. 155
Rosillo, Ronald H. 76
Rothrock, Irvin A. 228
Rutter, M. 261

Sadowsky, D. 188
Sager, Robert V. 263
Salamone, Paul R. 75
Santana, Rosina 314
Satow, Kay L. 94
Scriven, G. 218
Shapiro, D.S. 50
Shapiro, Esther 69
Shapiro, Howard L. 224
Shaw, Gavin B. 202
Shinn, Eugene B. 87
Shurka, Esther 130
Shwachma, H. 93
Silvers, S. 191

Simon, Ellen Perlman 87
Siski, D. 124
Sitarz, Annaliese L. 85
Sommer, Patricia 25
Starr, Clark D. 89
Stein, Joseph M. 109
Stephan, Cookie 145
Stirnkorb, Mary 151
Stodden, Robert L. 150
Stokes, Janet 115
Strauss, Helen M. 115
Sullivan, Neil V. 150
Svec, K.H. 301
Swanson, Donna 51

Tal, Y. 55
Thompson, Clare W. 212
Thompson, H.M. 301
Thornton, Larry W. 41
Tolor, Belle 287
Tomblin, J. Bruce 101
Turner, Patricia 137
Tyler, Nancy 137

Udelman, Mary Lou 297
Uhlig, George E. 291
Uyehara, Katherine 323

Van Demark, Ann A. 299
Vash, C.L. 133
Victor, James B. 102
Villenewve, C. 260

Wahl, Priscilla 198
Warfield, Martha 34
Weinblatt, Eve 263
Weiner, Irving B. 200
Wernstock, Carol L. 139
Wieder, Daniel 110
Wilcox, Robert D. 193
Willerman, Lee 155
Williams, D.E. 321, 322, 328
Williams, Gwendolyn K. 283
Williams, Judy 313
Williams, Susan M. 135
Wilson, Frank B. 142
Winter, S.T. 55

Wolff, James A. 85
Woolf, Gerald 68
Worden, J. William 273

Yamamoto, Kaoru 285

Zalkind, S.S. 248
Zerega, W. Dennis 295
Ziegler, Edward 153
Zimmer, Catherine H. 269
Zimmerman, Irla Lee 323
Zyzanski, S.J. 120